TIME LOOP

SEEING AMERICA'S FUTURE
IN
PERSIA'S PAST

CHAIM BENTORAH

All Scripture quotations, unless otherwise noted, are from the King James Version of the Bible.

Time Loop: Predicting America's Near Future Through Persia's Ancient Past

Cover and Interior Page design by True Potential, Inc.

ISBN: (Paperback): 9781953247148

ISBN: (e-book): 9781953247155

LCCN: 2020947817

True Potential, Inc.

PO Box 904, Travelers Rest, SC 29690

www.truepotentialmedia.com

Produced and Printed in the United States of America.

Darius I image included in cover montage: https://commons.wikimedia.org/wiki/File:Tomb_of_Darius_I_Image_of_Darius_I.jpg#filelinks

CONTENTS

INTRODUCTION

In Geneva, Switzerland, there is the Large Hadron Collider (LHC) with a nine billion dollar budget, over 10,000 scientists worldwide, hundreds of universities and laboratories, and more than 100 countries contributing to its research. Many physicists are hoping that this massive undertaking will help answer some of the fundamental questions in physics which concern the basic laws governing the interaction of forces on a subatomic level; that it will explore the deep structure of space and time and the relationship between quantum physics and general relativity. General relativity describes the universe on a visible scale. Quantum physics tells us about how things work on the unseen level of atoms and subatomic particles, the building blocks of our physical world.

Quantum physics is becoming a popular pastime with many Christians, mainly because, for once, science seems to be dovetailing with Christian beliefs. In his book, *Time Loops and Space Twists, How God Created the Universe*, Fred Alan Wolfe, an American theoretical physicist specializing in quantum physics and the relationship between physics and consciousness, explains how our understanding of time, space, and matter has changed in just a few short years and how it can give us a glimpse into the mind of God. "Let there be light," now takes on new meaning as quantum mechanics (the math proving quantum physics) proves how everything needs light. He speaks of Time Loops and Space Twists.

Quantum physics has captured the imagination of Christians. Several theories have captured the attention of Christians like myself. For instance, everything in this physical realm made up of what we call matter is composed of the same thing. As I write this, I am sitting in a chair by a desk in a building. We are all made of the same thing, subatomic particles. The difference between my desk and my physical body is just how the particles are arranged and vibrate. Everything in the universe vibrates. Sound, light, and energy all vibrate. We learn in Genesis 1:2, *"And the Spirit of God moved upon the face of the waters."* The word "moved" in Hebrew is *rachaph*, which means to flutter, shake, or vibrate. Could it be that God vibrated the world into existence and saw that it was good? The word "good" in Hebrew is *tov*, which means to be in harmony. To be in harmony is when vibrations are in sync with each other. When man sinned, he fell out of harmony with God. God had to send His Son to die on the cross to bring us back into harmony with Him.

A spirit is energy, and according to the law of physics, energy cannot be destroyed. Our physical bodies are out of harmony with God; hence they are decaying. One day we will have a new body that will vibrate on God's frequency, so to speak, resulting in a body like the original Adam had in the Garden of Eden before the fall. This body will be immortal and live forever. Our spirits are or were out of sync with God until Jesus Christ, God's Son, made an atonement for our sins to remove that sin and put our spirits back in harmony with God. It is a choice given to man; if he wishes to be in harmony with God, he need only ask. If he doesn't, God will not ask, but when the man dies, his spirit leaves his body. A spirit is energy, and according to the law of physics, energy cannot be destroyed. That spirit, or energy, has to go somewhere. If it is not vibrating on the same wavelength as God's, it will go to a place where those vibrations are in sync with something other than God's. I don't have to tell you where that is.

Quantum physics suggests the possibility of multiple universes giving us a picture of God creating a personal universe for each one of us. Only He and you exist in your universe, but that universe is capable of interacting with other universes. This personal universe makes it possible for you to have a personal relationship with God; a universe where God does not concern Himself with anyone but you. Since God does not live in time and time only exists in this natural world, God is free to move back and forth through time and the billions of different universes. Yet, as quantum physics hopes to prove with the Large Hadron Collider, a particle can exist in two places at the same time. In other words, existing in the past and present at the same time or in another dimension. That other dimension might suggest the realm that the enemy lives in. We can call it another dimension or another universe.

Dr. Wolf speaks of time loops and space twists. The term time loop or temporal loop is used as a plot device in fiction where a character repeats a span of time or an experience in hope of breaking out of the cycle of repetition. However, a time loop may also be referred to as a causal loop, which is unchanging and self-originating.

Dr. Wolf has his own definitions of time loops and space twists. I developed a different variation on the definition of a time loop and space twist, which does differ from Dr. Wolf. However, he did give me the inspiration for my own theory as to what Daniel meant in 12:4: *"But thou, O Daniel, shut up the words, and seal the book, [even] to the time of the end: many shall run to and fro, and knowledge shall be increased."*

Rather than use Dr. Wolf's term *space twist*, I would like to use the word, *corkscrew*. This idea of men running to and fro has fascinated many Bible commentators. I would like to apply the terms time loop and space twist in a much simpler fashion. When I say time loop, I am speaking of events in time repeating themselves.

George Santayana (1863-1952) said, *"Those who cannot remember the past are condemned to repeat it."* We have been repeating the past over and over throughout history. As I worked on my Ph.D. in Biblical Archaeology, I was amazed at how it seemed that the past was always repeating itself. I also noticed that similar events throughout history occurred more frequently as time advanced. Dr. Wolf talks about the relativity of time and how time passes differently according to one's situation in the cosmos. He uses an example from Eastern religion, which teaches that Lord Brahma lives for one hundred years. Twelve of his hours consist of one thousand cycles of four ages called Yugas, which corresponds to 4,320,000 solar years. Time is relative to the kind of body one occupies. While Brahma's one hundred years equal 311 trillion of our years, an insect's one hundred years might come to no more than one of our days. The point Dr. Wolf was making is that time and space are no longer absolutely separated in spacetime. All time is relative. Indeed, science can now prove that intervals separating observed events can be as long or as short as one might imagine depending on how the observers of these events are moving relative to the speed of light and to each other.[1]

This fact made me think of such verses in the Bible as II Peter 3:8:

> *But, beloved, be not ignorant of this one thing, that one day [is] with the Lord as a thousand years, and a thousand years as one day."* Or *Matthew 24:22: "And except those days should be shortened, there should no flesh be saved: but for the elect's sake those days shall be shortened.*

In the Aramaic, the word shorten is *kara,* which comes from the root word *kar,* which is a word for grief and sorrow and is also an adverb for the word, whenever. It has the idea of time being shortened. How can you shorten time unless time is relative?

---

1   Wolf, Fred Alan Ph.D., Time Loops and Space Twists: How God Created the Universe, Hierophant Publishing, 2010 Pg. 4

The lifespan of a human is much greater than it has ever been in history, so how could time be shortened if we live longer. My theory is that people lived to be hundreds of years before the flood, but God shortened man's life after the flood because life was very grievous and sorrowful. Yet, in a relative sense, we are still living as long as people before the flood because time does not exist in God's realm. We may be living to an average of 75 years, but before the flood, before God shortened time, it would be the same as 750 years.

This shortening of time is where I get my corkscrew theory. A corkscrew starts wide at the bottom, and as you move upward, the space in the screw becomes narrower. In God's fashioning of time, He made it like a corkscrew. Initially, there was a wide gap between one level of the corkscrew to the next. Hence, I would give my definition of a time loop as a repetition of events from one period of time to the next. Now apply this principle of the corkscrew. You have one event on the first level of the corkscrew repeating on the second level repeating to the third level repeating to the fourth level, and so on. However, as each event repeats itself, the distance between each level gets narrower. As we approach the top level of the corkscrew, or the end of times, that event which used to repeat itself every tenth generation is now repeating itself within one generation. Hence you have the expression, *men running two and fro*, from one event to the repeated event within their own lifetimes.

Jesus said in Matthew 24:6-7:

> *And ye shall hear of wars and rumours of wars: see that ye be not troubled: for all [these things] must come to pass, but the end is not yet. (7) For nation shall rise against nation, and kingdom against kingdom: and there shall be famines, and pestilences, and earthquakes, in divers places.*

Have there not always been wars and rumors of wars, famines, pestilences and earthquakes? How can that be a sign of the end? I believe Jesus is referencing the corkscrew idea of time. As time reaches its end, events in history will repeat themselves much quicker through each generation, until they repeat in one generation, as men run to and fro from one event to a similar event in one lifetime. My father used to say there was usually one war for every generation; today we experience several wars in just one generation. God is shortening time; and we are reaching the tip of that corkscrew to the end of time.

As a student of history, I see many events of our ancient past repeating themselves. The ancient Persian Empire introduced freedom of religion, diversity of culture, and honored the Jewish people. I see history repeat itself with the United States as a modern Persian Empire that introduced freedom of religion and diversity of cultures to the world. Persia was one of the first empires that did not ransack and strip a nation of all its resources when they conquered it. Just as the United States did not ransack the nations it conquered but emptied its own treasuries to restore the conquered nation. The parallels between the Persian Empire and the United States are uncanny, to the point of aiding the Jews in their return to their homeland.

Suppose this theory of history repeating itself is true.

Suppose this theory of history repeating itself is true. In that case, just as the Persian Empire did, there will come a time when internal conflict, a decline in world power and influence will come, causing the United States to back away from Israel. There will arise leaders who oppose Israel just as there arose kings in Persia who would eventually oppose Israel. By that time, Persia was no longer a world power. Is that the fate of the United States? Do we see history repeating itself right now? Even in the coming year?

Let me state emphatically, I am not a prophet or a watchman. I have no supernatural insight into the future. I am only a scribe, a student of history, and ancient languages, working on a crazy theory of time loops and corkscrews in time. I do, however, believe we are seeing a definite turn in direction as a nation. I believe the past year's events are a clear indication that we have reached a crossroads. The choices we make in the next few months will determine which timeline this nation will follow. Will it continue on the path of the ancient Persian Empire to decline, or will we follow the path of Nineveh and repent, resulting in God sending a great revival and granting us a lengthening of time. I do not believe the future is set in stone. I believe there are at least two timelines. If quantum physics has anything to say, there be many possible timelines, depending on the choices we make.

If quantum physics has anything to say, there be many possible timelines, depending on the choices we make.

Let me share one more point. Throughout this book, I reference someone I call the enemy. I am referring to what Christians call Satan. However, in the Bible, the word *Hasatan* simply means the *accuser*. The use of the definite article Hei means that this is not a proper name but only a regular noun. If Scripture would not give the old buzzard the dignity of a proper name, then neither shall I. So I will just refer to him as the enemy. Occasionally I will use this proper name, not to give him that respect, but to remind you of to whom I am referencing.

1

The Mighty Persian Empire 550 BC to 330 BC

Persia is a Greek and Latin pronunciation of the old Persian word, *Parsa*. It was a country dating back to around 1000 BC, located in a region in Northern Mesopotamia, which today includes North-Western Iran and the Zagros Mountains. For many centuries they were ruled by the Neo-Assyrian Empire (911-609 BC). The Persian Empire is also known as the Achaemenid Empire. Achaemenes is believed to be the father of Teispes, who is an ancestor of Cyrus II (Cyrus the Great) and Darius I. Many historians believed Darius I made up the whole story of Achaemenes to justify his position in Persia's royal line. If there was a line of Achaemenes, Darius was likely not a part of that family. But he was a true patriot of Persia and admirer of Cyrus. He believed Cyrus's successor, his son Cambyses, was not being true to the principles laid down by Cyrus and had weakened the empire. Darius wanted to seize the throne in order to make Persia great again. Darius succeeded in doing this, even though he was an outsider who upset the whole nation when he seized power and practically caused a civil war.

Our story begins with Cyrus, the Great, who ruled the Persian Empire from 559-530 BC. He was a fearsome but benevolent ruler who championed human rights and respected the culture and religions of the people he conquered. In 539 BC, he conquered the city of Babylon and brought an end to the Babylonian Empire. Within the next nine years, he transformed Persia into the known world's mightiest empire.

Cyrus left his son Cambyses II as governor of Babylon; an office he held for only nine months. For unknown reasons, he was removed from the position by his father. For the next eight years, Cambyses II sort of bounced around Babylon as a prince of Persia, plotting his next move. During this time, likely around 536 BC, Daniel had his vision and visitation from the messenger from heaven in response to Daniel's prayer to understand his vision. The messenger was delayed 21 days being "withstood" by the prince of Persia. After delivering his message, he went off to fight with the prince of Persia, prophesying that the prince of Greece would soon be coming.

Six years later, in 530 BC, Cyrus died in a campaign at the North East frontier, and Cambyses became the sole ruler of Persia. History gets a little foggy at this point, but the commonly accepted story is that Cambyses' brother, Bardiya, was the legal heir to the throne.

He began to worship the goddess Neit who was supposed to be the creator of mankind and the world. When the Persian Empire was at its peak of power Cambyses immediately set out in conquest. He should have stayed in Persia to shore up his kingdom, but instead invested much of Persia's resources into conquest, reducing Persia's might with much internal conflict. Cambyses ruled for eight years and spent little time in Persia. He spent most of his time in Egypt, which he conquered, and was busy adopting much of its culture. He began to worship the goddess Neit who was supposed to be the creator of mankind and the world. She was a terrifying goddess of war and child slavery. After eight years, Cambyses returned to Persia only to discover on the way back that an outsider, a member of his guard, named Darius, staged a coup and put none other than

Cambyses' brother Bardiya, who was the legitimate heir, on the throne. Here again, is where history gets a little foggy. Cambyses was seriously wounded in the thigh on his way back to Persia. He was either wounded in battle, or the wound was self-afflicted in a suicide attempt. He died a few days later but supposedly confessed on his death bed to having killed his brother, and that the Bardiya sitting on the throne of Persia was an imposter. This could not have worked out better, as Darius now started to declare the same thing: Bardiya was a fraud. His name was Gaumata, a magician and priest. Darius staged another coup, murdering Gaumata and either fabricating his own story or presenting some evidence that he was of the royal family of Achaemene, the legitimate ruling house. He assumed the throne of Persia after the report of Cambyses's death.

This was likely an act of God, as Cambyses would have established the Egyptian religion and the worship of the goddess Neit as the state religion, eventually preventing the Hebrews from returning to the Promised Land.

As can be expected, Darius, upon assuming the throne, faced much opposition from the former ruling party. Most claiming he was not a true heir to the throne nor a member of the royal family. However, Darius set to work draining the swamp, so to speak.

However, Darius set to work draining the swamp, so to speak.

a member of the royal family. However, Darius set to work draining the swamp, so to speak. This made those from the former ruling party upset, and all the more determined to have Darius removed from office. They made numerous attempts to have him dethroned.

Miraculously, Darius overcame all attempts to have him delegitimized and removed from office, which was a good thing because Darius, although a real rascal and street fighter, carried out much of King Cyrus' mandates on human rights and religious freedom, restoring the greatness of Persia and paving the way for the return of the Jews to their homeland. He also started causing a cold to hot to cold to hot war with Greece, which may explain why the messenger to Daniel's next battle was with the prince of Greece. God needed to keep Persia mighty until the Jews made their way back to the Promised Land.

Darius and his principles of rule continued for 36 years; however, he died before implementing all of his goals, among them to completely restore the temple of Jerusalem. Upon his death, his son Xerxes I, or as he is known in the Book of Esther, Ahasuerus, took over the throne. He, of course, was Esther's future husband.

As I said, history is a little foggy. The parallels I am going to make may not be based upon complete historical accuracy. Many legends surround the Persian Empire. However, there is good historical evidence for the timeline presented.

2

Daniel and His Visitor

But the prince of the kingdom of Persia withstood me one and twenty days: but, lo, Michael, one of the chief princes, came to help me; and I remained there with the kings of Persia. (20) Then said he, Knowest thou wherefore I come unto thee? and now will I return to fight with the prince of Persia: and when I am gone forth, lo, the prince of Grecia shall come.

Daniel 10:13 &20

As I indicated in the last chapter, history is a little foggy surrounding the timelines. There may be commentators who disagree with my timeline. I am only using the generally accepted timeline. However, I need to caution; I had a professor who said that facts in Archaeology change every twenty-five years. Some new discoveries could prove my timeline to be in error.

In Daniel 10:1, we read:

In the third year of Cyrus king of Persia, a revelation was given to Daniel (who was called Belteshazzar). Its message was true and it concerned a great war. The understanding of the message came to him in a vision.

If we assume this third year means the third year of the reign of Cyrus, this would put the year at 556 BC as Cyrus's reign began in 559 BC. However, if we put it at the start of his reign over

Babylon, this would date it at 536 BC as he was established as the King of Babylon in 539 BC.

I would consider 536 BC to be the most likely date, if we consider the prince of Persia to be an actual person rather than a demon or a fallen angel. I believe the prince of Persia, as mentioned in the last chapter, was Cambyses II, who was in a transitory state at this time and likely plotting his next career move. This would also make sense in the idea of doing battle or warfare on an angelic level.

God commissioned a heavenly being to personally bring this understanding to Daniel in a vision.

Daniel 10 has many interpretations and explanations. The reason this passage has so many different explanations is that it is beyond our understanding. Daniel is now under Persian rule, after the fall of the Babylonian Empire. He had a vision of 70 weeks, which troubled him, and he was seeking an understanding from God. In response to his request, God commissioned a heavenly being to personally bring this understanding to Daniel in a vision. This being was most likely an angel; some say Gabriel. Some believe it was not an angel but was Jesus. However, this is pure speculation; we don't know who or what this heavenly being was.

He was commissioned to go to Daniel the same day Daniel prayed, but he was "withstood" twenty-one days by the prince of the kingdom of Persia. It is uncertain if this was a spiritual being or an actual prince of the Persian Empire. What is important for this discussion is that there was some sort of spiritual battle taking place. This spiritual battle is what we need to understand if we are to understand what is happening in the United States today.

There have been many teachings regarding spiritual warfare, and I have no idea which, if any, of these teachings are accurate. Some teach that there are territorial spirits, evil spirits that are assigned certain territories. Some teach that angels are constantly in a fight with demons. In this case, this spiritual being had to hurriedly give his message to Daniel so he could rush off to do battle with the prince of Greece.

I don't know about you, but, from the sound of things it appears God cannot control His creation. He has to build an army of angels to defend His empire. He is so busy juggling the universe that He hasn't the time to deal with our little problems. He has a team of subordinates to handle the load. They don't seem to be very effective if it took twenty-one days and the Archangel Michael's intervention to overcome a simple prince of Persia.

Another thing that bothers me about warring angels is how can they be defeated. Do they get wounded and sent to an angel hospital to recover? Do they just vanish when struck by an angelic sword as in a Frank Peretti novel? What kind of weapons do they use? Doesn't a sword seem a bit old fashion? If God is so powerful and in such control, why does He allow the fight to go on? Why not call an end to it before some angels get hurt?

Finally, what is the purpose of this warfare to begin with? Does the devil believe he can defeat the Almighty God, his own Creator? Did God create a Frankenstein monster that was capable of destroying its Creator?

Satire aside, there is only one thing that God will not exercise control and power over. To do so would defeat His purpose in creation. That is to control a human being's will. The human race must have complete control of its own will. Man's control over his own will gives the enemy an opportunity for an even playing field.

God could create any being he wanted, and create that being to love Him. Yet, the very nature of love demands a choice. For love to be love, one must choose to love. God cannot force a human being to love Him. To do so would defeat the very nature of love.

> *For we wrestle not against flesh and blood, but against principalities, against powers, against the rulers of the darkness of this world, against spiritual wickedness in high [places].*

Ephesians 6:12

In the Aramaic, this would read: "*For your conflict is not against flesh and blood, but it is with principalities, rulers and with the world's power of this darkness and with the wicked spirits under heaven.*" This would suggest that wicked spirits influence our rulers. The spiritual warfare is a battle of wits with God's angels trying to influence someone to do that which is in harmony with God. The minions of the devil are trying to influence the person in the other direction. It is sort of like the old cartoon of a pitchforked devil standing on a man's shoulder whispering in one ear while an angel stands on the man's other shoulder, whispering in his ear: "No, don't you do that." The final decision is left with the man himself. If we look at spiritual warfare in this light, it would mean that the prince of Persia would have to be a reference to a natural living human being and not a supernatural being.

In other words, our battle is with the forces of evil trying to influence us to surrender our wills to them rather than submitting our will to God. During Daniel's time, Persian rule was in flux, and Persia went through several rulers in a very short time. It was a crucial time that would determine Israel's fate of returning to their land in the future.

The enemy knows he cannot defeat God's plan, but he can influence many to turn away from God, to choose evil rather than good, that is, to choose that which is not in harmony with God. The Book of Job is the picture of the role that the enemy is playing. His challenge was that Job was not serving God out of love, but because of all the benefits. Take the benefits away, and he will choose not to serve God.

What gives the devil the audacity to think he can defeat the Almighty God, his own Creator? The enemy is not out to win the war, only as many battles as he can. Jewish wisdom teaches that the devil is a *Yetzer Hara*, a tendency or inclination to do evil by violating God's will. The term is found in Genesis 6:5, *"yetzer lev ha Adam ra,"* which means the imagination of man's heart is evil. The Talmud in Succah 52a teaches that the greater the man, the greater is his evil inclination. Traditional Judaism believes that this *yetzer hara* is not a demonic force but a misuse of things the physical body needs to survive.

In Deuteronomy 11:26, God tells Israel just before entering the Promised Land, *"Behold, I set before you this day a blessing and a curse."* God gives us a free will, a choice. He gives only blessings, but we have the choice to use those blessings to be in harmony with Him or turn them into a curse by bringing us out of harmony with Him. God's blessings can be turned into a curse; it is our choice. The *yetzer hara* is constantly battling to violate the will of God. The desire for food can lead to gluttony. Certain medications can relieve pain; a blessing. But these medications can be abused; a curse.

There are certain groups of Jews who do believe in the personification of the *yetzer hara*. The Dead Sea Scrolls, in apocryphal books such as the Book of Enoch, speaks

The *yetzer hara* is constantly battling to violate the will of God.

of fallen angels. The Talmud itself in Bab Batra 16a speaks of Satan, the *yetzer hara* and the Angel of Death as the same. There are other passages in the Talmud which do not deny the external existence of Satan. However, the emphasis is on the *yetzer hara*, the evil inclination, and the enemy playing on the evil inclination to turn God's blessings into a curse. These evil forces have one goal, which is to cause mankind to fall out of harmony with God. Yet, God has placed within us the ability to choose His blessings and use them to be in harmony with Him. However, evil and good influences cannot force us in one direction or the other; they can only create events or manipulate desires to influence our choices.

My father used to tell me the story of an old Native American who was also a Christian. Someone asked him what it was like. He said it was like two dogs inside of him fighting. One good and one evil. When asked, *"Which one wins?"* He replied: *"Whichever one I feed the most."* Call this evil force a *yetzer hara*, a demon or the devil does not matter. It amounts to the only weapon the enemy has, and that is to influence us. It is the same weapon of defense that God's messengers have, the power to influence us.

When we offer prayers of intercession, we are sharing our will, our desire for God to intervene.

The ammunition they use is our will. When we offer prayers of intercession, we are sharing our will, our desire for God to intervene. God cannot intervene and force man to change his will. In Exodus 32, we read how God decreed that he would destroy Israel and make a new nation from Moses. Israel had surrendered to their *yetzer hara*, and there was no way God could interfere with their wills. He gave them a free choice, and they chose the curse rather than the blessing. God's only recourse was to remove Israel and start over again. But Moses interceded on behalf of Israel. He exerted his will that they be spared, and when he did, we read in Exodus 32:14, *"And the LORD repented of the evil which he thought to do unto his people."* The word repent in Hebrew is *nacham*, which means to change an attitude, but its Semitic root comes from a word which means to let out air, to breathe out, in other words, to give a sigh, like a sigh of relief.

Moses gave God the ammunition He needed to defeat the *yetzer hara*, Moses' will. That is, the power of intercessory prayer is our wills that we are giving to God when we intercede. It was Daniel's will and the will of his friends praying that commissioned the messenger to come to him with understanding. However, it took twenty-one days of using the power of those wills to battle against the wills of the *yetzer hara* to finally influence Cambyses to move in the direction God desired.

The war that is fought in the spiritual realm is a war of influence. It is a battle to manipulate the will of the human being. As we watch riots taking place in our country, people scratch their heads, wondering how the radicals think they can get what they want through destruction and violence. People wonder how these radicals think that they are serving their cause through violence. They are only creating more hatred and anger.

In the spiritual realm, the target is not the government, the social system, or the establishment. The target is believers. The enemy wants the media to focus on hatred, violence, and anger. The enemy wants the believer to see the carnage and bloodshed

> The enemy wants to get our goat, to arouse a passion of anger and hatred, the very ammunition he needs to win the battle of evil over good.

resulting from hate and anger. I have heard dedicated believers talk about what they would do if they got their hands on those "punks." They would show them. They would teach them a thing or two. All the time, the enemy is laughing his way to the Bank of Human Wills. Loading his weapon against God with the will of believers directed toward his agenda of hate and anger. Christians are playing right into his hands. Why is there so much evil happening? The enemy wants to get our goat, to arouse a passion of anger and hatred, the very ammunition he needs to win the battle of evil over good.

This is where the real battle is taking place in the spiritual world. This is how it is fought in the spiritual realm. It is not of flesh and blood but of rulers and with the world's power of this darkness and with the wicked spirits under heaven."

The word principalities in Aramaic is *arakus*, which is a word for judges and officers. The word ruler in Aramaic is *shalata,'* which are wicked, corrupt, godless powers who control a nation. These could be governmental, business, educational, and even religious powers that are corrupt and godless.

"... against powers, against the rulers of the darkness of this world." In Aramaic, the word, power, is *'achidi*, which comes from a root word *'achad*, a unity in strength that is simultaneous and in unity with another force. Darkness is the word *chashak*, which is a thick darkness that encompasses someone. The powers of darkness are a supernatural force that not only encompasses someone but empowers them as well.

Ephesians 6:12 tells us that we wrestle with wicked and corrupt people who have the power or authority of a political, educational, business, or religious office that they can exercise over us to accomplish the goals of an evil supernatural power from darkness. It is a force opposed to the Light of God, to accomplish purposes of evil.

Christians are convinced that all will be resolved if their political party rules this country. Christians are also divided over which political party that is. Families are being divided and destroyed. Christian children are rising against Christian parents over political differences. Never has there been such polarization between political parties.

The enemy has taken off his mask. He has succeeded in confusing evil for good and good for evil. It is okay to destroy a shopping district to steal goods you cannot afford. After all, insurance will pay for it. It is okay to physically attack someone who opposes your viewpoint because they are too stupid to see what is right, and you need to make them realize how wrong they are. They may even believe it would be alright to take someone's life if that person opposes their viewpoint; if that is the only way to establish their belief system.

As the coronavirus pandemic begins to subside, we will reach an intense conflict between those who insist we open up our economy and those who believe we must keep it closed. Some will argue that we are killing people by opening up the economy, causing the virus to resurge, while others argue that many more will die if we don't open the economy. I am watching Christians becoming very emotional over this topic, literally breaking relationships over it and even falling into hatred. Ultimately, both sides are playing right into the hands of the enemy, who only wants to create an atmosphere of hate.

Spiritual warfare has and will continue to intensify. Hate will grow stronger; conflicts will not end after the election. It does not matter who gets elected. The enemy has declared war on the American church. We need to know who are enemy is and what our weapons and defenses are. This country's real fate lies not in the election results but in the purging and restoration of the American church.

Never before in American history has the church wrestled with these powers as they will in the coming months. For many years the church had the upper hand. We controlled Hollywood. They were careful not to create movies that were offensive to our Christian values. After World War II, the moral code in Hollywood started to change with Howard Hughes producing a movie which Christians found offensive. They rallied together but were not successful in closing the movie down. From that point forward, there was a push to gradually rebel against Christianity and what they called censorship. Comedians like Lenny Bruce, who brought vulgarity into standup comedy, are today considered martyrs for taking a stand against the church.

For many years, we had our way. People respected our faith. They would clean up their language and apologize if they said something offensive. Ministers, pastors, and priests enjoyed a high social status and respect in the community. Today they are looked upon as predators. Believers no longer have the upper hand; we are now the underdogs. Darkness has overtaken the nation's system, and it is our fault. We demanded that the government do our jobs. We wanted laws passed to fight against vulgarity, abortion, and immorality. Many states had laws that made it illegal; one could be sent to prison for committing adultery.

Darkness has overtaken the nation's system, and it is our fault.

It was not the government's job to regulate the nation's morality. It was our job. It was our job to introduce Jesus Christ, not legislation. We were too lazy to share our faith, the love of Jesus Christ, and the gospel of His salvation. We somehow had the idea that if we were a nation who followed God's moral laws, even if it was through civil laws that forced people to act morally, God would find favor with us.

But, if you look at Israel's history in the Bible, you will find that it was not the gentiles' wickedness who brought the nation down. It was the compromise and hypocrisy of the Children of Israel that brought the nation down. Our job was to deal with wickedness through the gospel of Jesus Christ, not put a Band-Aid of civil legislation over it. The heart needed to be changed. Was it the thieves, the robbers, the prostitutes, the lawbreakers that Jesus condemned? He loved them and forgave them. It was the religious leaders that he called vipers and dogs. The religious leaders knew the Word of God but twisted it for their gain and benefit.

I don't blame the unbelievers; they are tired of being bullied by the Christians, being forced to behave like Christians when their hearts are unclean. Now that they have the upper hand, laws are being passed that will make us the martyrs like we made Howard Hughes and Lenny Bruce.

Laws against hate crimes and hate speech have been passed. They are being interpreted and modified so that even sharing the gospel with someone that finds our faith offensive could end up being a crime. Under these hate laws, churches could be forced to take down their crosses, hide their Bibles in public for fear it will offend someone, and bring legal action against us.

This nation does cherish its religious freedom. It is unlikely we will experience persecution like certain nations in the world. But what we will face will be far worse.

Had Cambyses succeeded in his return to Persia and turned the worship of Neit into a state religion, the Jews would have experienced untold persecution. However, Daniel fasted and prayed, and God sent a messenger to influence the prince of Persia. The enemy had his influencers as well; and it took the presence of the Archangel Michael to tip the influence in God's direction, sparing Israel from a persecution unparalleled in their history. The history of Persia's respect for religious freedom protected them from outright capital punishment for worshipping God. Still, the enemy, with people like Haman in his pocket and ministers who plotted against Daniel, causing his visit to the lion's den, would have been in greater numbers. They would not have to resort to tricks and lies to persecute the Jews. They could have Jews eliminated for just being Jews. But the prayers of men like Daniel and his friends gave God's messengers the power needed to defeat the spirits of darkness.

3

The Power of Prayer and Fasting

Daniel and his friends knew the power of prayer and fasting. What was this power? People seem to think that their prayers will change God's mind or that God will not act until He has a certain amount of people praying. I don't know the reasoning behind this thinking. Does God have an accountant angel in heaven with a quill pen, scrolls, wearing a visor, and writing by candlelight recording every prayer? Then every so often, God turns to this accounting angel and asks: *"Well, how many people are praying for old Chaim Bentorah?"*

"Not good," responds the accounting angel. *"That poor fellow just cannot generate enough prayers to get his answer."*

"How many more people does he need praying for him to get his answer?" Asks God, hopefully.

The accountant angel pulls out his pocket calculator and crunches some numbers. *"For his type of prayer and the answer he needs, at least a hundred more people praying for him are needed before you can answer his prayer."*

God walks away, shaking his head. *"Too bad, too bad, I kinda like the old guy, pity he just can't meet the quota of prayer for me to give him an answer."*

Yet, the Bible talks about the power of prayer. Look at Esther, who had the whole nation of Israel fasting and praying for her. Is that what it takes to get an answer? Do you need to hit Social Media to get everyone praying for you, hoping you reach some quota to persuade God to answer your prayer? Maybe the urgency or type of request requires a certain number of prayers.

I remember, as a child, we had what was known as Green Stamps. As an incentive to purchase from someone's store, they would give you little green stamps that you pasted in a book. For every dollar you spent, you got a certain number of green stamps. A catalog listed all the items; from fountain pens to refrigerators. The fountain pen only required a few books filled with stamps. The refrigerator required maybe a few hundred books filled with stamps.

Is that the way it is with prayer? Does each prayer represent one prayer stamp? Does a church full of people praying represent a full book? Does a city praying for one person mean a few hundred books? Then God has an angel check a catalog asking: *"Well, old Chaim is praying for some money to purchase a new printer. How many books of prayer stamps does he need?"*

"Well," says the catalog angel; *"A dozen or so people praying ought to do it."*

Or maybe God says: *"I just got an urgent prayer from Old Ben, he just had a stroke; how many prayers does he need to get healed?"*

The angel thumbs through the catalog: *"Let's see broken toe, diabetes, cancer of the liver, wow, a stroke requires more than cancer of the liver. Wait, here it is, Oh, boy. How many likes does Old Ben have on Twitter? He may have to tweet them."*

What is the power behind prayer, anyway? Do we have to bribe

God with prayers? Do we have to plead and beg, hoping He will feel sorry for us? James 4:2 says, *"You have not because you ask not."* Yet the very next verse says, *"You do not receive because you ask wrongly and spend it on your own passions."* (ESV)

What is going on? It is a war, a battle that is being fought on a spiritual level using spiritual ammunition. Sometimes you are your own enemy. The ammunition, as mentioned in the last chapter, is your will and the will of others. A will can be in harmony with God, and a will can be out of harmony with God. If the will you are releasing to God is selfishly motivated, not in harmony with God, don't expect an answer. If your will is in sync with the will of God, in harmony with Him, He can answer that prayer.

So, what about the idea of getting people to pray for you or for our nation? That is where the enemy sends in his influencers, and God sends in his influencers. Say some scientists are working on a vaccine for COVID-19. These scientists may be believers or non-

> Each prayer gives God's influencers more power to be influenced to search in the right direction, to find the right formula for a vaccine.

believers like the prince of Persia. It doesn't matter; what matters are the spiritual influencers and their ability to influence in their direction. Some do not want a vaccine; they want to see the pandemic and evil continue for their own political or personal reasons. They send their desires or wills to the enemy because that is compatible with his desires; he does not want a vaccine either. Then there are those releasing their wills to God to see a vaccine. Each prayer gives God's influencers more power to be influenced to search in the right direction, to find the right formula for a vaccine. Those whose desires are to see the plague continue are exerting their will to influence the scientists to search in the wrong direction.

Let's put this on a national level. Christians are so fearful over who becomes president that they overlook the power of prayer. It doesn't matter who the leader is. Cambyses was a royal rascal, but the messenger from God, with the help of the Archangel Michael, influenced the old buzzard to follow a direction that God wanted. But the power to influence and counteract the negative influence laid in the prayers and fasting of the saints.

Esther had people pray and fast, so the king would do a simple act of extending his scepter. That simple act of extending or withholding a scepter determined the fate of a nation. You can bet the enemy had all his minions trying to influence the king to withhold the scepter, which would have been the end of Esther. However, there was a nation praying and fasting. The power of the saints' will gave the messengers of God tremendous power to overcome the will of the enemy and his ammunition suppliers.

God just doesn't listen to our prayers. He uses our prayers to turn them into one big blockbuster of a bomb of positive wills that he throws into the face of the enemy.

Our nation's fate rests in the hands of the saints of God, not who gets elected to that office.

Our nation's fate rests in the hands of the saints of God, not who gets elected to that office. God can use either candidate to accomplish His purpose, but to accomplish His purpose, he put within us the power to do it. He uses our wills, wills that we give over to him, our power of choice that He can hold up to the enemy, and say, *"You lose. My people just overpowered you with their will, their right to choose good over evil."*

4

CAUSING SOMEONE TO SIN IS WORSE THAN MURDER

Numbers 25:16-18: *"And the Lord said to Moses Attack (Vex) the Midianites and strike them dead. For they assailed you deceitfully when they seduced you in the matter of Peor."* (Berean Bible)

Matthew 18:6: *"But whoever causes one of these little ones who believe in Me to sin, it would be better for him if a millstone were hung around his neck, and he were drowned in the depth of the sea."*

While preparing for a Torah Portion Study, I ran across a profound statement in the Midrash Rabbah: *"The one who causes a man to sin is even worse than the one who kills him."*

Freedom of Religion is one of our most cherished freedoms. It is very unlikely that freedom of religion will be outlawed in this country. There are some out there who would like it to be outlawed, but they are on our society's extreme radical fringes. They can make a lot of noise, but even a true atheist would be hard-pressed to deny someone the right to worship as they please. They may ridicule and mock believers, but they know religion is just too powerful in this country to outlaw it. I am not saying it is impossible; there could be a catastrophic event that would close churches, or a nuclear war, with martial law declared. But the enemy is not that desperate to close down religion. The enemy loves religion. It is a natural instinct in man to want to worship, to believe in a greater power, and Satan is okay with that. He has been using it to his advantage since the beginning of time.

The enemy has no problem with you attending church, so long as you don't go over the edge.

The enemy has no problem with you attending church, singing "I like God" songs, and getting all whoopee so long as you don't go over the edge. He will allow you to have just enough religion to feel you met your quota of goodness to slide into heaven. Recite prayers, quote Scripture verses, keep your mind on the football game you are going to watch after the service is okay, so long as you don't pause and think: *"Oh wow! God, you are so wonderful, I just love you so much."* That is taking it too far for the enemy. It is okay to imagine you're getting a touch from God; just don't try to hug Him.

George Whitefield graduated from Oxford and ordained into the Anglican church. He could not, however, find a parish. The formal, elite church did not welcome him. Calvinism was powerful in those days. The belief that only the elect would get to heaven was common. For many, the elect were the wealthy and influential people. The poor or lower class could not be the elect; if they were, they would be wealthy and influential, they would show the blessings of God. Churches made the poor feel unwelcomed and usually reserved a few seats in the back for the poor, if any at all.

Whitefield had this remarkable idea that God wants to save everyone, even the poor, and that the gospel should be shared with all people regardless of their social rank. He also had this idea that one could have a personal relationship with God. That sent shivers down the spines of the church leaders. I mean, it was okay to talk about the love of God but don't get too close to God. He is, after all, the Almighty and All-Powerful. Why, if people could have a deeply personal relationship with God and God could speak to everyone, what good would the clergy be? If people could study the Word of God on their own and reach their own understanding, then you would have all kinds of beliefs. No, a personal God was dangerous. People would no longer need the clergy to tell them what God wanted them to do.

So, George Whitefield took the Wesley brother's invitation to go to America and preach to the simple farmers, craftsmen, laborers, and, gasp! - Native Americans. The result was the Great Awakening and the start of a revival. People were experiencing a close relationship with God. Contrary to the religious elite's wishes, churches were springing up all over the land and growing. There were camp meetings where people were, oh my gosh, getting exciting about God, and loving God, and loving each other, and lives were being changed.

People from all over the world who were persecuted for their faith began to hear about this new land where you could worship God any way you wanted. Suddenly, people were flocking to America in search of the new thing called religious freedom. To be sure, there were other motives to come to America, but freedom of religion was right there upfront. All the time, the enemy was biting his nails, working overtime, trying to stop this onslaught of people seeking a personal relationship with God.

He started to succeed, not by trying to close the church, but by corrupting the church. He resorted to his age-old tactic called pride. If religion was popular, then so could the leaders become popular. In many cases, the only people who could read or write were the local ministers. They established schools and seminaries to train the religious leaders, doing the same thing as the religious leaders over the ocean, getting education, degrees, positions of prestige, and power. Young people saw the clergy as a way to become respected and honored, and all they had to do was get an education and preach a sermon once a week. The rest of the time, they could strut around the community accepting honor and respect.

If the leaders do not have a personal relationship with God, how can they lead their congregation to a personal relationship with God?

Of course, all this honor and education respected the very personal relationship with God out of the church leaders. If the leaders do not have a personal relationship with God, how can they lead their congregation to a personal relationship with God? It is like a bald barber telling you how to save your hair.

As this nation went through two world wars, a pandemic in 1918, a Great Depression in the 1930s, and then untold prosperity in the latter half of the 20th Century. God became a thing. Religion was something everyone did to be a good citizen. No politician would dare say he or she was not a good Christian. People wanted to be Christians because that was the nice and proper thing to be. All you had to do was go to a building on Sunday, endure some music that was not your style, and sit through a thirty-minute commercial from the preacher. Then you could declare yourself a Christian. Easy as pie. No need to sacrifice, no need to suffer any persecution, just a few minutes on Sunday, and you're bound for glory.

All the enemy had to do was settle the leadership down, make sure they did not preach on sin, and that offensive place called hell. I would often tell my Bible College students to not listen to what a preacher says, listen to what he does not say. What he says is beautiful and lovely. Love others, respect your neighbors, treat everyone equally and nice. All good words. The enemy likes those words, preach love all you want, just don't preach the blood of

Jesus, the penalty of sin, the need to have a Savior in Jesus Christ.

Reward the leadership with honor. Give them television appearances, boost that ego with invocations in local, state, and national government. Let them meet and even advise political leaders and lead them in prayer; just don't lead them to Jesus.

Reward them with excellent salaries to purchase nice cars, a second home, and all the blessings of this land. After all, they deserve it; they have an education and a position of power. What a shame if a pastor has to clean the toilet in the church or vacuum the carpets, how dare a congregation make their pastor do such mundane work.

Just make sure they do not preach the blood of Jesus, sin, sacrifice, surrender, and a personal, loving relationship with God.

In Exodus 15:9, we learn that the Egyptians and Edomites advanced against Israel's people, murdering them. Yet, God said you shall not abhor an Edomite nor an Egyptian. In Numbers 20:18, we learn that the Midianites and Moabites formed an alliance against Israel and tried to curse them through the pagan prophet Balaam, only whenever he opened his mouth a blessing came out. A donkey even tried to talk some sense into Balaam, who did not heed the advice. It is a sad day when you don't take the advice of a talking Donkey.

Knowing it was useless to try and curse Israel, Balaam suggested that King Balak of the Moabites send in Moabite and Midianite women to seduce the Israelite men. Balaam told King Balak that the God of Israel hates that kind of stuff, especially when it leads to pagan worship. They assume a foreign culture like the Moabite or Midianite culture. The results were pretty quick. The Israelite men were adequately seduced and began to worship and join themselves with the Baal Peor. Now the nations of Moab and Midian only tried to corrupt Israel, not murder them like Egypt and Edom. Yet God commanded that Israel not abhor Egypt and Edom, but for Moab and Midian, they were to attack or *tsarar* them and strike them dead. I will explain this play on *tsarar* later.

As for the Moabites, God declared in Deuteronomy 23:4: *"An Ammonite or a Moabite . . . even to their tenth generation shall not enter into the congregation of God."*

The Midrash teaches that from this, we learn that someone who causes a person to sin does worse than killing him, for one who kills him kills him only in this world. In contrast, one who leads him into sin will keep him from developing a close intimate relationship with God.

Jesus pretty well taught the same thing in Matthew 18:16.

But whoever causes one of these little ones who believe in Me to sin, it would be better for him if a millstone were hung around his neck, and he were drowned in the depth of the sea.

The word in Aramaic for little one is *zo'ra'*, which comes from a Persian word for little or diminished, tender, and loved. On the negative side, it means to belittle and humiliate someone. Only the context will tell you if you use the positive or negative definition. It sounds like a child, but it is not a word for a child, although it could be. It is used to describe someone who is childlike, innocent, and easily manipulated. The word for "better" as it is better to have a millstone around your neck is a play on words. The word in Aramaic is *paqach*, which is something used for profit or personal gain. It is rendered as better in the sense of bettering oneself. In this case, there is a little play on that word; it would be a profit or better to have a millstone tied around your neck and dumped into the sea and drowned. As a play on words, it describes the motive for causing a tender-hearted one who is inclined to God to sin; the motive is profit.

38

Jesus is speaking to those leaders, the ones who teach those who are hungry for God and long to build a relationship with Him. These leaders will teach doctrines that work to their advantage and profit. To draw in more offerings, or to attract more people to make them look successful. These are the ones who use their new converts to fill their wallets and make them look like spiritual giants, who build big churches and ministries just to make a name for themselves.

Note the words of Jesus, *"And he were drowned in the depths of the sea."* Did I tell you what happened to the Egyptians who tried to murder the Hebrews? You know the story, they were *"drowned in the depths of the sea."* Jesus was using a story very familiar to the Jewish people. Telling them, *"The Egyptians tried to murder your ancestors, but God was merciful to them; they were not abhorred, they just drowned in the sea."* Those who cause a spiritually hungry person to stumble, faces something much worse. They will be vexed.

Those who cause a spiritually hungry person to stumble, faces something much worse. They will be vexed.

The word vex in Hebrew is *tsarar*, related to the Aramaic word *zo'ra*, humble or innocent. This word, however, also has a negative side to it, to humiliate and shame someone. Before Israel was to smite the Midianites and Moabites dead, they were to first humiliate them.

We have all heard of famous Christian leaders who had made themselves rich off the backs of naive Christians, and then fell into a scandal that forced them to resign in shame and humiliation. Many often die not long after their *tsarar,* humiliation.

The Egyptians just died for murdering the Hebrews; no humiliation beforehand. The Midianites and Moabites not only died but suffered humiliation. Someone who causes a person to sin, to fall away, even to just stumble does worse to him than one who kills him.

What we have witnessed this past year is the stage being set for the revenge of the ungodly. Finally, after two centuries of being relegated to the ranks of outcast and the country's fringes, they have now achieved the upper hand. They can now unmask themselves and show their evil and have their evil is called good. Isaiah 5:20: *"Woe unto them that call evil good, and good evil; that put darkness for light, and light for darkness; that put bitter for sweet, and sweet for bitter!"* Never before in this country's history have we seen this verse become a reality as it has today; and it will continue to grow in intensity.

In the minds of the ungodly, the legal system is justified in shutting us down because we are haters, committing a hate crime.

The tragedy is that the church faces the temptation to compromise to win the acceptance of the godless. History tells us that this will naturally lead to a time when the church will be forced to accept what the ungodly demands. They will be forced to hide their Bibles, stop their gospel messages over radio, television, and social media, all in the name of censoring hate speech. We are seeing the beginnings of our gospel message being called hate speech. In the minds of the ungodly, the legal system is justified in shutting us down because we are haters, committing a hate crime.

Whose fault is it? It is ours because we have been too lazy to take the gospel message out ourselves. We have been too lazy to study the Word of God ourselves. Instead, we have used our wealth to hire preachers to do it for us. Unfortunately, many do not share our love for Jesus. They have been planted by the enemy to get us to use a watered-down gospel, so when the time comes, the enemy can easily lead us into a position of compromise. We used our power and influence to make the government enforce our ethics. We took advantage of our position and power in this country to force people to live our standards. Now that we are losing that power, they will use their power to force us to accept their standards, and the enemy will then apply his greatest tool – fear.

We have seen that the one who leads another into sin is worse than a murderer because the murderer only kills the body, which is temporal. The one who leads to sin kills the soul for eternity. The enemy is not interested in killing us off; there is too much danger of our embracing God. He would prefer to just slowly but surely corrupt us spiritually to draw us away from God.

No matter who gets elected to office, don't be afraid of losing our freedom of religion in the next year. Our concern should be that we will be enticed to draw away from God through intimidation and fear, forced to turn to apostasy to appease those who hate us and compromise to protect our freedom.

5

Beware of the Qlippah

Exodus 8:32: *"And Pharaoh hardened his heart at this time also, neither would he let the people go."*

Hebrews 3:7-8: *"Therefore, as the Holy Spirit says: "Today, if you hear His voice, Harden not your hearts, as in the provocation, in the day of temptation in the wilderness."*

Ultra-Orthodox Jews have a word from Classical Hebrew that I find very appropriate in this study. I will not use the word in the context that the Jewish people use it, and I hope they would not be offended if I use it in a Christian context. I would like to use the word in a singular form, *qlippah*. It simply means a shell or husk. It is a hard covering.

We have the story in Exodus, where Moses is trying to persuade the Pharaoh to let the Hebrew people go to their homeland. Initially, Scripture says that Pharaoh hardened his heart. Other passages say God hardened Pharaoh's heart, but that is another study. This study deals with someone who intentionally hardens his heart. There were occasions in which Pharaoh actively hardened his heart, and the Apostle Paul, in his letter to the Hebrews, also warns against hardening one's heart.

The word harden in Hebrew is *kavod*, which is the word for glory. It is used in the sense of heaviness or weighing down. It the context of hardening your heart, it has the idea of weighing it down with so many cares and desires of this world that you cannot hear God's voice. We are warned by the Apostle Paul to not harden our hearts. The word in Greek is *sklerynete*, which is in an aorist subjunctive active voice, second person plural from the root word *skleruo*. The aorist subjunctive indicates a finality. *"Do not by any means make you heart stiff; it may be the last time God speaks to you."* You and you alone are responsible for putting a *qlippah* or hard shell around your heart. It is an act of your will to block out the voice of God. The Aramaic uses the word *qasha*, which is also in an active voice. *Qasha* means to harden by creating difficulties. That is putting obstacles in one's path to make it more difficult or harder to reach your destination. Its Semitic origins have the idea of a storm at sea that keeps a ship from reaching its destination. I sense in my spirit, there is a storm coming that will create a *qlippah* or shell around the hearts of many believers in the next year.

It means to harden your heart, to allow barriers to build that make it difficult for God to reach your heart. You fill your heart with lusts, selfish desires, concerns, and fears, which create a *qlippah*, a hard shell that God cannot penetrate.

I have been watching a National Geographic series about people who live above the Arctic Zone. They go fishing when it is 40 degrees below zero. They chop a hole in the ice, then scoop out the slush until the water under the ice is exposed. They quickly put a baited hook and line into the hole because the water almost immediately freezes up. It is a continual process of scooping out the slush, or if they wait too long, they must chop the ice again, as it completely freezes over in just a matter of minutes.

I read how one rabbi described our relationship with God. During the week, we are concerned with the matters of this world, relationships, earning a living, maintaining shelter, and dealing with all the other worldly cares. During that time, a shell or *qlippah* begins to build up around your heart toward God. You are continually scooping out that slush with daily prayers and Bible study, but sometimes that slush turns back into ice and covers your heart. On the Sabbath, we are commanded to do no work, that is, not to engage in activities that will allow that slush or ice to build around our hearts. The Sabbath is the day we chop through that ice, remove the slush, and let God throw in his bait and hook to draw out from our hearts the benefits of love for Him.

The Farmer's Almanac predicts a colder than the average winter in 2020-2021. I thought that was a perfect metaphor, or sign, that we are approaching a time in this nation where darkness will send a chill throughout the land. It will be a deep freeze that we have not yet known. Believers are going to struggle harder than ever to keep that slush and ice from building a *qlippah* over their hearts. **Many Christians are getting used to not going to church as social distancing continues, and the Sabbath day is becoming like any other day of the week.** The fears, struggles, and persecution that believers will face will intensify, and the ice around many believers' hearts will thicken. Just as ice fishermen scoop out the slush to keep fishing, so we must always be on alert to make sure that the *qlippah*, or shell around our heart, does not harden from our worldly concerns and fears.

Prayer, studying God's Word, fellowship with God and with other believers will become more important, lest we allow the media reports of riots, killings, and hatred fill our hearts with fear, worry, anger, and hatred in return. Without this, we fall right into the enemy's plan to destroy our relationship with God.

We are responsible for allowing our hearts to harden. We are drawn to the news media and social media like a moth to flame. We read about all the hatred and evil in the world. We grow bitter over the unbelievers' hypocrisy who claim to be loving and tolerant but will not love God nor be tolerant of those who do. We then call our Christian friends and relatives and have a feast day of disgust, venting our hatred over the evils we see in the news media. We enter into arguments with our brothers and sisters over the perceived blindness of those who support a presidential candidate different from the one we support.

We grow angry, wondering how our Christian brothers and sisters could support a presidential candidate who displays such non-Christian values. We think they are stupid or blinded or just plain sanctimonious. *"How dare they think they are such loving Christians and cannot even see what I, the enlightened one, sees in the candidate I support."* Arguments between Christians ensue, relationships are broken, while all the time, the enemy is putting both parties in his back pocket.

The enemy is not going to destroy this nation with riots, unrest, or civil war. He is just going to create enough riots and unrest to get you angry enough to build that *qlippah* around your heart. He will expose blatant hypocrisy to create such disgust that the slush around your heart begins to turn to ice. He will keep churches closed or limit the congregation size due to social distancing. It will be just enough that you get used to not celebrating the Sabbath, and allow that ice to harden. Then he will pick you up and toss you into his bag of conquest, and by next year at this time, you will be just another trophy on his shelf.

6

Shibboleth

Judges 12:6 *"Then said they unto him, Say now Shibboleth: and he said Sibboleth: for he could not frame to pronounce [it] right. Then they took him, and slew him at the passages of Jordan: and there fell at that time of the Ephraimites forty and two thousand."*

In Judges 11, we learn how the Ammonites and the Israelites who settled in the land of Gilead, consisting mostly of people from the tribes of Manasseh and Gad, got into a land dispute. Israel rightfully owned the land through conquest, and now the Ammonites wanted the land back. I know it sounds a lot like today with the demand that Israel return to the borders before the Six-Day War. It was the same scenario. Israel just wanted to live peacefully, but the people of the land Canaan did not want them there, they went to war, and much was the bloodshed. When the smoke cleared, Israel had conquered additional territory vital to their defense. Then the prior owners of the land began to demand it back, saying it was rightfully theirs. The Gileadites declared, much as Israel is declaring today, *"Hey, this land is rightfully ours bought with the blood of our people. We desire no fight with you but if you insist on taking what is ours, then put up or shut up."* Unlike Israel's enemies today who have neither *put up,* nor *shut up,* the Ammonites decided to *put up.*

The Gileadites needed a leader, and the one best qualified was not their first choice. Jephthah was an outcast because his mother was a prostitute, and his father could have been anyone. Because of his questionable parentage, he was forced into exile and not allowed to live among his own people. Yet, he gained a reputation as a fearless warrior and leader of men. So, with tails tucked, the Gileadites came crawling to Jephthah, begging him to build an army and fight against the Ammonites. Jephthah agreed, so long as they would pay him a little respect and make him their leader, not only during the fight but afterward as well. They agreed, and Jephthah sent out the call to all the surrounding tribes to join him in battle against the Ammonites. Everyone who received the call responded except for the tribe of Ephraim that lived across the Jordan.

We do not know why Ephraim did not join into the battle with their brothers from Gilead. I suspect they just thumbed their righteous nose at Jephthah, calling him a bastard, which was quite correct. He was the son of a prostitute, after all. They would not join themselves to such a loser. God would surely not use such a person to bring victory; he did not have the right heritage.

He was an outsider, and surely, God could not use a man like him to fight for us. Back in 2016, we had several Republican candidates who fit our Christian values. It was assumed that the Democratic candidate did not fit our Christian values, so Evangelical Christians' hopes lay with the Republicans. As the contenders in the Republican primaries fought for the nomination, Evangelical Gileadites watched in dismay as their favorite candidates supporting their Christian values began to drop out. This left them with a Jephthah to fight for their values. With tails tucked, these Gileadites went to our modern-day Jephthah and supported his candidacy. But there were many Ephraimites who refused to support their Jephthah; after all, he did not display our Christian values. He was an outsider, and surely, God could not use a man like him to fight for us. He just did not have the right heritage. I mean, he cannot even quote Scripture correctly; saying, *"One Corinthians"* rather than the true believers who say *"First Corinthians."*

But apparently, neither side understood the *heart* of God and what God would do for someone who humbled himself before Him and was willing to give Him full credit for any victory. When someone does that, their past or heritage means nothing to God. So, God gave Jephthah a great victory, and he won the election. Ephraim knew they had made a big mistake by not joining with their brothers in a righteous cause when that happened. They went to Jephthah, and rather than apologize for their arrogance, they simply demanded to know why Jephthah did not ask them for help. Bad mistake. Jephthah knew he begged for their help, and Ephraim knew he begged for their help, but they were too arrogant to admit they were wrong. Their pride would not allow them to lower themselves to a man who was the son of a prostitute. Jephthah did not stand around and argue; he just lifted his sword, and the Ephraim-ites took off running, high tailing it toward the Jordan River. The only problem was that when they reached the Jordan, Jephthah's men were guarding the bridge. When the Ephraimites asked to be allowed to cross the river, Jephthah's men simply said: *"Sure, but first say the secret word."* They then asked what the secret word was, and Jephthah's men said, *"Shibboleth."*

> When someone does that, their past or heritage means nothing to God.

Now *Shibboleth* could mean either an ear of corn or a stalk of grain, but it could also mean a stream or river. In this context, it would most likely mean river and what Jephthah's men said was, *"Go ahead say the words, 'let us cross the river.'"* The problem was that even though they spoke the same language, they had a different dialect. The people of Ephraim did not use the letter Shin which made a *sh* sound. They used the letter Sine which made the *s* sound; so what they said was *sibboleth*. This mispronunciation immediately identified them as Ephraimites, and as a result, they were killed by Jephthah's men.

What bothers me about this is that they killed 42,000 Ephraimites using this little test. Now it takes time to kill 42,000 men, and I doubt very much they came to cross the river one at a time. They came in groups, and you would think that they would get wind of what was going on somewhere along the line and that they had better start practicing their *sh* sound.

I don't think the Ephraimites were that stupid. I think they were that arrogant, and they were not going to let the followers of a bastard tell them what they could or could not do. I think many of them deliberately said *sibboleth* as a challenge and died for it. Shibboleth means *a stream or river*, but the word *sibboleth*, when spelled with a samek, which also an *s* sound, means a *porter*. I believe the Ephraimites' arrogance led them to sneer back the Gileadites, calling them *porters,* who should help them carry their bags across the river.

In our society, the politically correct thing is not to question one's past or heritage.

Is there a lesson in that for us today? Many commentators will say that this whole situation between the brother tribes was one of pride. I agree and would render this whole story in that context. In our society, the politically correct thing is not to question one's past or heritage. We have come to respect single parents who manage to raise their children alone and the children from a single household who manage to overcome the difficulties and make something of themselves. But arrogance still thrives, and it thrives in our Christian communities.

You may have noticed that I have taken a lot of liberties with Jephthah's story in making a present-day political parallel. I believe I am correct in my interpretation of this story. Still, I have rendered this story from my heart, not my Ph.D. or my years of teaching and studying Hebrew. Yet, few people will challenge my interpretation because I have some *credentials.* My education and teaching experience are my *Shibboleth*. I hold up my diplomas, and I am allowed to pass with my interpretations of Scripture, no matter how wacky it is.

But I am also seeing *Shibboleth* being played out in the political arena. Evangelical Christians being hotly divided over the character of their president, who is a Jephthah. When I ask someone why they are voting for a particular candidate, I am constantly hearing how they do not like the other candidate's attitude, character, or behavior.

When I ask someone why they are voting for a particular candidate, I am constantly hearing how they do not like the other candidate's attitude, character, or behavior.

How could any Christian support such a person? No one mentions the candidate's platform or what he stands for; they do not vote for the guy because they just don't like him personally.

That is fine; it is their right as a citizen to vote for whoever they want or like. What I am talking about is the candidate's password or *Shibboleth*, which is his character. If a brother or sister in Christ focuses on the candidate's character and ignores his platform, they risk hurting their relationship with another brother or sister in Christ. It also works the other way around if one focuses on the candidate's platform but ignores his character, they will still be condemned for supporting Jephthah and allowing anger, even hate to ensue between both parties, destroying the relationship between one's spiritual brother or sister. All the time, the enemy has both in his greasy palms.

This is where the problem lies, not in who is running for president. God can use whoever is president to accomplish His purposes, remember Cambyses? With enough prayers and releasing of the wills of God's people, He can influence even a Cambyses to make decisions that will conform to His will. The problem lies in the conflict between brothers and sisters, the destruction in the family of God over a *shibboleth*. Because of a dispute and disgust over the character or heritage of a leader rather than acknowledging their true leader to be God, they let arrogance, smugness, and sanctimonious feelings lead to anger, hatred, and division, destroying what God meant to be something good. God never intended for 42,000 people to die over such a petty dispute.

Once again, we see a time loop with history repeating itself, now in this nation. It is not the violence in the streets, the riots, and the pandemic that we need to focus on, that we can pray about. Where our focus needs to be is on God and loving our brothers and sisters even if they do not say *shibboleth* right. If we don't, the results will be bitter, painful, and damaging to the Church of God in Jesus Christ. The enemy knows that the greatest weapon against the riots, violence, and pandemic is the love of God, and the enemy is working overtime to destroy the foundation of that love in God's Church. Christians, who are the bearers of God's love, are the only hope for this country. The enemy has us on his radar and is about to launch a missile of hate at our weapon of love.

7

THE MA'APILIM

Numbers 14:40,44: *"And they rose up early in the morning, and gat them up into the top of the mountain, saying, Lo, we [be here], and will go up unto the place which the LORD hath promised: for we have sinned." (44) But they presumed to go up unto the hill top: nevertheless, the ark of the covenant of the LORD, and Moses, departed not out of the camp."*

When I was in my second year of seminary, I heard two Old Testament professors discuss a topic I always wondered about. I was shocked to discover that their knowledge of this clearly biblical episode was so limited. They were discussing God's judgment against Israel by being denied entrance to the Promised Land because of the report of the ten spies to not enter the land. One professor commented to the other: *"I think they did make a few attempts to enter the land."* The other professor replied: *"Yeah, I think they did."* I'm thinking: *"Say what? These are professors of Old Testament teaching graduate-level classes on the Old Testament, and they are not sure if there was an attempt to enter the land?"* To be fair, after 45 years of studying the God's Word, I am still finding things in the Bible that I didn't know were in there.

Keep in mind that I grew up in a very fundamentalist Bible-believing church and attended church practically every day of the week. We had a Bible Study and prayer meeting on Wednesday.

We had a club program where we studied the Bible and memorized verses. We attended church twice on Sunday, morning worship and evening service, and of course, we had Sunday School, which was totally Bible-centered. This, as well as belonging to a Bible Club (Youth For Christ) while I was in High School. After high school, I attend two Bible Colleges, then seminary (a repeat of Bible college) and graduate school, and spent four years working on a Ph.D. in Biblical Archaeology. Now you would think after all these years of Bible training, I would have heard of the *ma-apilim*. I didn't. We hear a lot about the *Nephilim*, which covers fewer verses than the *ma'apilim*. Yet, the message of the *ma'apilim*, I believe, is more important.

The word *ma-apilim* means the defiant ones. The story of the *ma-apilim* is found in Numbers 14. Some Israelites tried to make amends for failing to enter the Promised Land on the ten spies' advice, who said that Israel did not stand a chance of conquering the land.

Less than twenty-four hours after the spies report and God's declaration that *this generation would not enter the Promised Land*, a group of Israelites repented and said: *"We're ready, let's go get 'em."* But God said, *"Too late, you had your chance."*

Maybe that is why we never hear this story. Is not God a God of second chances? If the people repented, would not God say: *"Okay, I understand, you're only human, now let this be a lesson to you and go out there and win one for the Gipper."* But God shut the door.

I believe there is an important lesson for us as believers in this story, and it needs to be told and preached. If we are born again, then we truly believe in God and His omnipotence. Yet, sometimes that belief is obscured by a spirit of foolishness. In admitting their sin, Israel demonstrated their belief in God's power; but it was too late. God had already decreed that the generation would die out before entering the land. In their zeal to repent, Israel went too far. Moses already explained that the window of opportunity had closed. They just did not listen to God; they listened to their own desires and will. They figured once they repented, all was okay, and they could move forward. They were wrong. They mistakenly interpreted God's discouragement as a test of their resolve. The *ma'apilim* **They mistakenly interpreted God's discouragement as a test of their resolve.** left that next morning without Moses or the Ark of the Covenant. They were full of faith that they would be victorious, only to have the Amalekites, Amorites, and Canaanites quashed their attempts and beat them back to Hormah.

They broke God's heart when they refused to enter the land. Eight of the ten spies reported in Numbers 13:31: *"We are not able to go up against the people for they are stronger than* **we.**" The Talmud teaches that the word *"we"* is '*oto* in Hebrew, a third-person singular and should be rendered as *"they are stronger than Him."* In other words, they said that the enemy was so strong that not even God could conquer them. The people listened to the report and agreed they were stronger than God, which broke God's heart. After all God did to prove his faithfulness and power, how could they say such a hurtful thing?

I thought of this story as we experienced the race riots. I live just a few blocks where the riots took place in my city. Businesses along Cermak Road are boarded up, stores were looted, and there is much hatred among the races. I have friends on both sides. I taught classes in the inner city. I drive through the inner city every day. It's not as bad as the media portrays. They like to focus on the crazies and their unrealistic demands. Still, the fact remains, many have been hurt and just as many who realize this and want to do something to atone for the sins of their fellow man. Maybe they want to shine someone's shoes. In their haste, they do it only to make themselves feel better or righteous. They end up making the offended parties feel even more violated than before through their patronizing. When we seek forgiveness, we must consider the injured party's needs rather than our own need to appear noble and forgiving.

When we've hurt someone, we must ask: *"What does the one I hurt need right now?"* The path to reconciliation is to listen closely to the one we've hurt and to genuinely seek his or her welfare. I see many *ma'apilim* in my neighborhood; they mean well, but they are not listening to the cries of those who they hurt. Just like the Israelites who meant well, who tried to make up for their lack of faith, but they just did not listen to Moses or God. They tried to do it their own way to satisfy their own needs and desires.

They insist that all we need to do is elect the right politicians.

Christianity in America has many *ma-apilim*, defiant ones. They insist that all we need to do is elect the right politicians. We spend our money and time working to get them elected. Then we see the giants of rioting, violence, and a pandemic. We realize that even electing the right people would not put an end to it. But we believe we might delay their conquest if we work to get the right people elected. So, we invest more time, effort, and finances to get someone to do the job God has called us to do.

The enemy blinds us to our country's history of revolt against a superior power and the great power of God, delivering us from the very beginnings of our country. During our Revolutionary War, we were outnumbered, outclassed, and out financed by a powerful nation, yet God delivered us. God delivered us when this greater power invaded our land and even burned the White House down in 1812. Yet, we came out of it experiencing a great spiritual revival, called the Second Great Awakening. Then there was a Civil War where 670,000 to 700,000 Americans were killed or wounded. God brought our nation through that. There was a little known revival where over 300,000 people from both sides of the war surrendered their lives to God. We came into the 20th Century, where God took us through a World War. A pandemic in 1918 followed the revivals lead by men like Billy Sunday and the Azusa Street revival. Then there was a Great Depression and a second World War. This was followed by a great awakening of 1947-1948 with the founding of para-church organizations like Campus Crusade for Christ and Billy Graham's massive crusades. There was a war in Viet Nam resulting in riots, both racial and political. This was followed by a revival called the Jesus Movement. Throughout our history, God has brought us out of deep trouble, some much worse than today, to lead us into that Promised Land of revival. Do you think the enemy is going to sit back and let another revival sweep across this nation? Don't kid yourselves. He is working right now to create his army of *ma-apilim*, defiant ones who are looking to our government, and not God, to save us.

Unless Christians wake up and realize that the government will not save us, only God will save us, we will miss that opportunity to enter the Promised Land of revival. God is, right now, setting the stage for this next revival. It will not only be a revival, it will be a reformation of the churches.

Like Joshua and Caleb, we must focus on the Promised Land of revival as God's gift after our struggle in this wilderness of pandemic, economic collapse, and unrest. If all we see are the giants that threaten us, we will miss our window of opportunity to usher in the next Great Awakening.

Each revival came when the Christians finally realized that the arm of the flesh would not save them; but only God could. This next revival will come when His people who are called by His name will humble themselves, seek His face, turn from their wicked ways of depending upon the arm of the flesh, and pray. Isaiah 7:14.

8

Your Eyes Will Fail You

Lamentations 4:17: *"As for us our eyes yet failed for our vain help, in our watching we have watched for a nation that could not save us."*

The sins of the people of Judah had finally reached their climax. For almost four hundred years, Judah went from periods of idolatry, to destroying idols and worshipping God, and then back to idol worship again. It was not that they abandoned God at any one time. The temple still existed, the people still celebrated the many feasts, and the priest still offered their sacrifices. But it was mainly for appearance's sake, or to fulfill a sense of duty. They were a religious people who had no heart for God. They worshipped God, but they also had other gods.

For over two hundred years, the United States has gone from periods of idolatry to revival; and from destroying idols to worshipping God, and then back to idolatry. We have always been a religious people and even called a Christian nation. We are a land of religious freedom with many churches. Still, much of the worship is for appearance's sake or to fulfill a sense of duty. This country is filled with religious people who have no heart for God. People who worship God but also had other god of prosperity, comfort, security, and national pride. Many times we've crossed that line from worshipping God to worshipping our comfort. As a result, God takes us out of our comfort zone. He allows a pandemic to create such fear that we are forced to shut down businesses and churches. He has allowed violence and riots to take place, creating even more fear, and yet, do the people turn to God or to the arm of the flesh to save them?

When Jeremiah gave God's warning of coming destruction, the people mocked him and said:

> *Oh, come on Jeremiah. People have talked about destruction for years, and look, we are still here. The temple still stands. We are the people of God. Do you honestly think God will destroy this building constructed in His honor? Do you think God will let His nation be destroyed? Look at our prosperity, security, and comforts. Do you think God would give us these things only to take them away?*

Many say it is a different world today than it was a year ago.

Yet, overnight, everything changed. We have experienced that to some degree in this country. Overnight we found that a disease has robbed us of our freedom to meet with others, worship together, and attend entertainment events. Overnight it robbed us of what we thought were secure jobs and healthy lives. Then, in the midst of that, we watched people's frustration pour out into the streets in violence. Many say it is a different world today than it was a year ago.

Is it possible that, like the nation of Judah, God is showing us where our hearts lay, and what it is that we worship? In Lamentations 4:17, we see where the hearts of the people laid. The Assyrians were ready to march on Judah. Instead of turning to God for help, they looked to the nation of Egypt to deliver them. Yet, Egypt had their own problems; they would not come to deliver Judah. The people placed their hope of salvation in the arm of the flesh.

Christians are worried sick over the next presidential election.

They are looking to the next president to save them. Do they honestly believe that one person's election will turn things around and bring us the peace, comfort, and security we long for? History has shown over and over that only God can bring about that peace. Our next president is an Egypt that we are waiting for and looking to deliver us.

The words. *"our eyes yet failed for our vain help in our watching,"* is a very sad picture. A clearer rendering would be, *"our eyes became exhausted watching for the help that never arrived."* We vainly watch the media for signs of hope and help to deliver us, but it only brings more bad news. We are exhausted, watching for help that never seems to arrive. The word failed is *kalah*, which has many possible meanings from a bride to destruction. *Kalah* here has the idea of becoming exhausted after putting every part of your being into something. The word vain is *haval* in Hebrew, which is a word used for a vapor. It is like a cloud, you can see it, but there is nothing substantial there when you walk into it. The word for watching is *sapah,* which is a watching and waiting. It is not just a watch like being on guard duty, but it is a watch filled with hope and anticipation. This is a picture of people facing destruction but clinging to the last bit of hope, until the last minute, when they believed God would send the Egyptians riding up to rescue them. The Egyptians never came. The Egyptians owed them. Judah was there to help the Egyptians in their time of need. The Egyptians had promised to help them. But such is the nature of trusting in the arm of the flesh.

I see Christians like the people of Judah looking and waiting for the next election, hoping that the next president will deliver them from the coronavirus, from their economic troubles, and from the unrest and violence they see in the news media.

61

The people pinned their hopes on the arm of the flesh to the very last moment, but the phone never rang. Their last hope of escape that they could see in the natural never materialized. But, we can't be too hard on Judah. Are we not doing the same thing, hoping for a vaccine created by man that will end the pandemic, an election that will swing in our favor? And if it never materializes, what will happen? When the arm of the flesh fails, where will we turn? Sure, we are the people of God; look at all the beautiful church buildings we built and support. Surely God will not allow us to be destroyed. Surely, at the last minute, the arm of the flesh will rise and save us. We have resources, contacts, talents, or whatever to fall back on to deliver us. Yet, all these are the arm of the flesh, and they can fail us.

God could have used the Egyptians to deliver Judah. There were any number of ways that God could have delivered Judah. That is the problem; we are deciding how God should save us. Perhaps we should consider a move like Jehoshaphat in II Chronicles 17-20, who faced total defeat, outnumbered by three kings who allied against him. Rather than seek the alliance of other nations or depend upon his own army's strength, he instead gathered the people together and fell before God. God responded with a battle plan that sounded ridiculous and should have gotten Jehoshaphat impeached for trying to implement it.

He called the priest and temple choir to stand before his army with no swords or weapons of any kind. He commanded that they march to the field of battle, singing and praising God. When they declared, *"His mercies endure forever."* God stopped the advance of the three kings and caused their troops to start bickering with each other to the point where killed each other off. When Jehoshaphat and his army arrived at the scene, all they found were dead bodies, many supplies, and no living army. They had all fled. Jehoshaphat did not suffer one casualty.

There are efforts today to draw Christians together to pray. Some even try to gather support from Christians to go among the rioters and share the gospel of Jesus. The few that have made this attempt have seen God do mighty miracles. We don't hear about them in the news media. There are just not enough involved in these attempts to catch the eyes of the media. But it seems the real reason we do not see more of this is that there is too much infighting and criticism among believers. That's a sure sign that people are not sincere about joining their hearts with God. They seek God only with their minds. They would rather tell God how to accomplish these ends while watching for the Egyptians, that is, the election results. They figure God will use the Egyptians or the next president to deliver them, so they pin their hopes on what they see and not on what was is unseen.

> **They figure God will use the Egyptians or the next president to deliver them, so they pin their hopes on what they see and not on what was is unseen.**

Jehoshaphat had no idea who God would use to deliver them. He knew God said they would not have to lift a sword. Perhaps Jehoshaphat felt that God would send some friendly army down to destroy the three kings. I am sure he did not expect God to cause the three kings to fight against each other.

Jehoshaphat set his eyes on God, not on what he could see. I Corinthians 2:9: *"However, as it is written: 'What no eye has seen, what no ear has heard, and what no human mind has conceived' -- the things God has prepared for those who love him."* (NIV) We cannot even begin to imagine what God will do to deliver us from this present circumstances. Yet isn't that what faith is all about?

Maybe we should stop telling God how we expect or would like to be delivered and just trust Him to come up with the solution. A rabbi once told me something that was life-changing for me: *"Faith is not obtained, it is revealed."*

Ephesian 2:8: *"For it is by his grace that we have been saved through faith, and this faith was not from you, but it is the gift of God."* (Translated from the Aramaic Bible, the Peshitta)

We have all the faith we need; it is just covered by that *qlippah* that ice that keeps getting thicker and harder the less we exercise that faith.

9

A Cottage in a Vineyard

Isaiah 1:8: *"And the daughter of Zion is left as a cottage in a vineyard, as a lodge in a garden of cucumbers, as a besieged city."*

This passage caught my attention because I am reading this as I eat my cucumber salad. Otherwise, it would probably go unnoticed as it does for most Christians. Its meaning seems obscure, but as I examined it I found it presented a very sobering thought for us, the church, and our nation.

The daughter of Zion is often a reference to Mt. Moriah, a small mountain located in the Old City Jerusalem. It is probably the most valuable piece of real estate in the Middle East, if not the world. It is the most hotly contested pieces of real estate in the world, to be sure. It is one of the most sacred places for Christians, Jews, and Muslims. Sitting on top of Mt Moriah is the Temple Mount, a 37-acre tract of land where the Jewish temple once stood. Today there are several important Islamic holy sites located there, which includes the Dome of the Rock.

In a figurative sense, the prophet says that the temple will be left as a *cottage in a vineyard*. The word *cottage*, although not an incorrect rendering, can be sort of misleading. It is the word, succah, in Hebrew. Many of you probably immediately recognize this word. When you hear it, you do not think of a *cottage* as we consider a cottage. When we hear the word *cottage*, we think of a com-

65

Time Loop

fortable little, sturdy house. However, when you hear *succah*, you think of a flimsy little booth that the Jews stay in during the feast of Tabernacles (Succoth). This is what is being referenced.

During a time of harvest, whole families would live in the fields or vineyards to do their harvesting. They would set up lightly constructed *booths or succoth* made of brushwood that they would live in to protect their fields from thieves and be near the field so they can begin their harvesting the first thing in the morning without having to make a journey to their fields each morning. After the harvest, the little shack would be left to face the elements and would gradually fall apart during the storms that would come over the year.

The word for *lodge* is *molown* in Hebrew, which is an *inn, an overnight stopover*. It was nothing more than a shelter where rather unsavory individuals would spend the night. It was a place where there was no privacy at all. You would sleep in a little loft above your mule or camel, and there would be a well in the middle of the various lofts. Everyone would have their own little campfire, and in the morning they would leave. As I said, it was usually inhabited by unsavory characters. It was not unusual to wake up in the morning and find your camel and supplies missing.

The prophet is saying that because Israel's rejection, God will abandon them, and their temple will fall into ruin, like a temporary booth set up during harvest time.

As I drive through Chicago's inner city, I often see the remains of old churches, either lying in ruins or converted into community centers. Just a few blocks from where I live is a small park recreational building. I recognize this building from almost half a century ago when I was a Moody Bible Institute stu-

66

dent. Back then, it was a little Bible church of about 20 people. One semester I attended that church and helped out in their Sunday School. It is now closed. The community turned the property into a playground and the building into a community center.

Every year 6,000 to 10,000 churches in this country close their doors. Many other churches merge or rent out spaces in their buildings to help the cost of maintaining the building. It is not unusual in my community to see a church building with two different signs announcing two different churches that meet in that building. It seems that when it comes to paying the rent, denominational barriers don't stand in the way.

Every year 6,000 to 10,000 churches in this country close their doors.

When I look at some of these churches, especially those in ruin, I cannot help but try to imagine the history of that church. How a proud group of Christians pooled their resources to establish this house of worship. How they sacrificed their time to teach Sunday School, Vacation Bible School, and run club programs to raise their children in the knowledge of God. I imagine the joy and celebration of each Sabbath when these Christians came together to worship, and then I wonder what happened. Why did the momentum stop? There are many reasons why a church does not grow and closes its doors. However, having grown up in an Evangelical church and spending my life in Evangelical churches, I can guess many of these reasons. Jealousies, infighting, gossip, and dissatisfaction over the direction a church would be going. Many leave because they just could not feel the joy of the Lord. They could no longer feel God's presence in the church, so they move to another church where they might enjoy an experience.

Many times preachers themselves contribute to the demise of the church. They see a lack of growth or even a decline in numbers, and they panic. They start preaching sermons on the dangers of going to hell if you don't attend church or tithe. Few do not say you will go to hell if you don't attend church; what they say are things like: *"I find it very hard to believe that a person can be a Christian and not attend church."*

Ultimately, the reason a church fails is that God's Spirit is no longer manifested. He is present, but because of the *qlippah* (hard shell) among the congregation, the Spirit of God cannot break through that hardened heart.

There is a secondary meaning behind Isaiah 1:8 as well. There is a gradual deterioration to the elements and/or a takeover by unsavory individuals.

Now they are like *booths in the field* that have been abandoned after harvest.

I have seen many believers, churches, and ministries that were once very cutting edge, dynamic, filled with the power and presence of God harvesting lost souls. Now they are like *booths in the field* that have been abandoned after harvest. They are deteriorating and they don't even realize it. They live on the glory of the past, but the presence of God is no longer there. No one is getting saved, and sermons on good things, love, and beauty replace the Word of God, so no one is offended. Even in Charismatic circles, I find they are trying to pump it up with a lot of shouting and fast music and make people think the presence of God still fills their booth. They try to portray that it is still harvest time, but in reality, the harvest is long past, the harvester has left, and their booth deteriorates. Yet, they dance around to the music and sing heart touching songs and say, "Oh, feel the presence of God, He is still here," but it is not the presence of God, it is just the effect of the music on one's emotions. Some churches prioritize hiring a full-time worship leader more for his musical talent that his relationship with God. In the backs of their minds, they think a good music program will attract people, particularly young people. You may attract people with a good music program, but that is no guarantee you will have a godly congregation.

In ancient times they burned fragrances and used certain essential oils to create a feeling of euphoria, a sense of peace, and tranquility. They would say, *"See this is the presence of God,"* but it was not the presence of God; it was only the effect of the fragrances upon the emotions. God's presence has long since left those churches or ministries which are in decline, but people do not realize that they substituted fragrances or music for the *feel good*. When the presence of God leaves, worldly devices fill the gap.

Worse yet, some are like the lodges in the garden. They are becoming filled with unsavory types. They are compromising with the world, trying to keep things going by using the world's marketing tools and the wisdom of the world. They take surveys of the neighborhoods to see what the people want and what will bring them out to their churches or ministries. They seek to attract the media with their good works to attract more people and finances. All the time, their *succah,* their booth in the harvest field, has been abandoned by God. The harvester has left the field.

We need to occasionally sit back and take a good look at our lives. We need to ask if our spiritual lives are not just empty abandoned booths. Are our *yahoos* and *praise alleluias* coming from a deep love for God, or are they just echoes of past glory? We need to consider if we are not sustaining ourselves through unsavory means. Maybe we are just playing worship music as the ancients burned oils or fragrances, to create that *good feeling* that was once the presence of God in our lives. We are saying our praises, loud prayers, and prophecies to convince everyone we are still in the midst of the harvest. But there lies within us unconfessed sins and a booth that has long been abandoned by God. He has moved on to harvest other fields.

69

With the events that have taken place this past year, I see another time loop; history repeating itself. I see a powerful storm coming at the church in America. The Talmud teaches that the Jewish nation is like a tree. I can make the same comparison to the church. A tree has roots; it has a trunk, branches, leaves, and fruit. The roots nourish the tree by drawing in the water and nutrients from the soil. If the roots are strong and firmly planted, the tree will be strong and bear luscious fruit. It will strengthen the tree's trunk, which will send out those nutrients through its branches and create beautiful leaves and a bounty of fruit.

The fruits are the converts that come into the church. Branches and leaves are those who bring in the new converts and encourage them, befriend them, and make them feel like they have a home. The trunk of the tree is the pillars of the church. They are the elite, the pastor, his assistants, the largest donors, and the talent who lead the worship team. Oh, and the roots? They are the Miss Bettys of the church.

Miss Betty is an actual person. I worked with her in a mailing room at a law firm many years ago. She was a lovely Christian lady who loved Jesus with all her heart, soul, and might. Everyone liked her. They did not mind her talk about Jesus at all; it was just a natural part of being Miss Betty. She had a childlike mind and was enraged over the announcement that the United States would seek to send men to Mars. I happened upon her during her lunch break when she was reading the newspaper about this announcement. She was livid. She declared to me: *"You see this? Why we go to Mars? What business is it of ours?"*

I started to pick up on her enthusiasm as I replied: *"That's right; we could use that money for many other things."*

She ignored my contribution to the conversation and just continue her rant: *"I say it is their planet, let them have it."*

"Right," I replied, *"It is their plan.... Huh? What? Whose planet?"*

She looked at me like she instructing a child in something very obvious. *"The Martians, of course; it's their planet, we have no business taking their planet. We will only bring the Martians to earth and enslave them. I say it is their planet, let them alone. You don't see them coming down here trying to take our planet, do you?"*

Well, I had to admit that I hadn't seen any Martians walking down Michigan Avenue lately.

I will tell you something. This same Miss Betty, who believed in unseen Martians and felt compassion for them, believed without question in an unseen God who heard her prayers and answered them. If anyone felt a need for prayer, the first person they would go to was not the educated pastor, who would laugh at Miss Betty's belief in Martians, it would be Miss Betty herself.

When the pastor prayed, God listened, but when Miss Betty prayed, God smiled. Her faith was unmoving. If any member of the worship team needed prayer, you would find them in Miss Betty's janitor closet, waiting for her to show up. They would get on their knees and ask Miss Betty to lay hands on them and pray her fervent righteous prayer because they knew that her prayer would rock heaven more than their Christian rock music.

The roots of a church are the Miss Bettys. They are often unseen, not very attractive, and pretty well ignored. But without their nourishing prayers, the pastor and his elites would lose their spiritual strength, the branches would wither, the leaves would die, and there would be no fruit.

It doesn't take a prophet to predict that when the storms hit, the first trees to go down will be those with no roots; the dead trees, the churches that are spiritually dead, and just existing off their past glories. The next trees to blow down will be the churches depending on its tree trunks for survival, having no praying roots like Miss Betty. But the churches that will stand firm and strong and bring revival to this land will be the churches filled with Miss Bettys. They may not believe in Martians, but they do believe in an unseen God and that God hears their prayers.

The tragedy is that most churches don't even realize they have no roots and are already dead. The enemy doesn't strike a church dead overnight. He gradually sucks the life out of it; turning it into what I call a zombie church, dead but still moving and wreaking havoc.

I would like to use that example of the frog who jumps out of a pot of boiling water. Some eighth-graders did this experiment, and it seems the frog is not such a dummy after all. He jumped right out when it got too hot. Unfortunately, many Christians do not have the sense of that old toad. They just sit there in the water until the heat of hell itself overtakes them. We drift away from our first love without realizing it. That is why we have a Sabbath to spend one day a week chopping away at the *qlippah* ice that has built up over our hearts during the week.

10

QUEEN OF HEAVEN

Jeremiah 44:17 *"We will certainly do everything we said we would: We will burn incense to the Queen of Heaven and will pour out drink offerings to her just as we and our ancestors, our kings and our officials did in the towns of Judah and in the streets of Jerusalem. At that time we had plenty of food and were well off and suffered no harm."*

Since the early 1950s, something new hit the mainstream of Christianity. It arose during the healing revivals that were popular back in that day. This seems to be an extension of the New Thought movement that started in the 19th Century, but it got its boost from televangelists and the Charismatic Movement. It comes by various names, *health and wealth gospel*, or *gospel of success*, but the most common name is the *prosperity gospel*. This is a belief that financial blessing and physical health are always the will of God, and that faith, positive speech, and of course, a generous donation to the cause, will increase one's material wealth. Follow the formula and you will enjoy financial security and good health. This gospel teaches that the Bible is a contract between God and man. If you have enough faith, God will deliver.

This teaching also emphasizes that the atonement includes not only forgiveness of sins, but such goodies as the alleviation of sickness and poverty. Sickness and poverty are simply curses that can be broken by faith.

To be fair, there were many in the Pentecostal and Charismatic movements, along with many mainstream evangelicals, who strongly criticized this new theology, calling it idolatry and exploitative of the poor. The last half-century is littered with the dry sunbaked bones of many of these teachers who crashed and burned in scandal.

It is not my role as a scribe to condemn any teachers, movement, or theology. I am not condemning the prosperity movement. I only wish to point out the dangers of taking a path down that road.

My first encounter with this theology was when I attended a fairly large church that started a building program. Their denomination sent in a top fundraiser. This old boy knew his stuff. He first preached a sermon showing how David heard about Goliath and the reward King Saul was offering anyone who would take Goliath's challenge. He read the scriptures where David went around asking what the reward was, and this preacher emphasized and slowly read the words: *"What is the reward that the King is offering?"* Then he said: *"You see there, even David had no problem with serving God for a reward."* After a few more Scriptures proving that God wanted us to be prosperous if we were willing to slay our giants, i.e., financial difficulties. This preacher had us stand up and announce what we were willing to donate to the building fund.

I didn't have much money. My secular job was just a stop-gap measure to keep me fed until I entered my real vocation as a pastor. So, with much great embarrassment, when my turn came, I just shook my head and turned to the next guy, who immediately announced his generous gift. There were no words of condemnation, but no words of encouragement either like *"I understand it is hard for some of you."* Then this preacher told the pastor that, next Sunday, he was to give everyone a chance to testify before the whole congregation of how God repaid their generosity.

Would you believe that by some coincidence, my supervisor got promoted at my secular job. They gave his position to me with a nice big $3,000 bonus. In those days, and my financial situation, it was more money than I ever had in one lump sum. The next Sunday, people stood to testify how God healed their headaches, bad backs, and how they had received the money they'd loaned out in the past. I thought, *"Blast it all, I have a testimony that would have brought the house down, except everyone knows I passed on the opportunity to get a blessing."*

I felt God whispering in my heart:

> *One day you will be writing books, make sure you include your testimony in one of those books, with this little message, you can't bribe God, I will bless who I want to bless, regardless of what they do.*

That day has come as I share this testimony with you. We are about to enter a time of testing where history will repeat itself.

We are about to enter a time of testing where history will repeat itself.

In 1420 the great plague pandemic known as the dreaded Black Death swept throughout Europe. It is estimated that the population of Europe was 80 million people. Around 50 million people died from the plague. More than half, about 60%, of the population died.

When the plague hit, the people turned to the church. The church responded by sending prayer warriors out to the villages and towns to pray over the sick. Many of them contracted the illness and died, and the plague just continued. The church, that bragged they carried the power and favor of God, proved to be powerless in the face of this plague. People faithfully continued to attend mass and tithe to the church in hopes that God would show favor, and spare them and their families. There was hardly a family that was not affected by the plague. By the time the plague subsided, many people had lost faith in the church and in God. By 1517 AD, Europe was ready for a reformation of the church. The church's corruption was widely known. The pain of the suffering from the plague was still keenly felt when a monk named Martin Luther challenged the authority of the church and started the great reformation and the Protestant movement.

We already see the beginnings of a financial crisis from our own coronavirus plague. Churches that boast they will not practice social distancing because God will protect them, suffer as members come down with the virus. 6,000 to 10,000 churches close every year in this country. That number will skyrocket as people get into the habit of not attending church due to social distancing, and not giving their tithes without an offering plate to coerce them. Some churches are claiming a drop in revenue by up to 65%.

However, when the smoke clears and churches re-open to full capacity, I believe we will see a very changed landscape. Many who embraced the prosperity movement will drift away like the people in the 13th Century, who depended upon the church to get them through the plague, and watched the church fail them.

I believe my experience over 40 years ago and the message God whispered in my spirit will come to pass. People will learn they cannot bribe God with church attendance, offerings, faith, and prayers. I am not saying that God does not appreciate church attendance, offerings, faith, and prayers; He just doesn't want it as a bribe.

Let's say a husband wants to go fishing with his buddies the same weekend his wife had special plans. So he comes home from work with a bouquet. He puts the flowers on the kitchen table and says: *"Okay, here are your flowers. I got the kind you like, now let me go fishing with my buddies this weekend."* Do I have to tell you where those flowers are going to end up?

Let's look at this another way. A husband has no plans to go fishing. He wants to spend the weekend pleasing his wife, and to top it off, he purchases flowers; the kind she loves. He comes home, kisses her, and says: *"Honey, been thinking about you all day and I'm looking forward to our weekend together. I wanted to find some way to show you how much I love you and, well, I got these flowers."*

Do you get the difference?

How many of us treat God the same way. *"Okay God, I gave you my tithe and my offerings. I have attended church every Sunday for the past year. I put up with all those same old sermons and that horrible music that goes on and on. I even did some witnessing and read my Bible and prayed for at least 15 minutes every morning. Now get me that new car I've been wanting."*

Do you honestly believe God is going to say, *"Oy, what good things you've done for me, Bunkie, here are the keys, go to Honest John and get your new car."*

How about waking up some Sunday morning and saying, *"Well, Lord, not too thrilled with this new music they have at church, but if others are blessed by it, so be it. I just want to be in your house, rejoicing with others and sharing your love. Got my tithe right here, I know you don't need money, but I can't think of a better way to just show you how I love you."*

I think you get my point; or rather, God's point. He gave me this message over 40 years ago, *"Tell them in your book that you cannot bribe Me."*

In Jeremiah 44:17, we read what the people of Judah, who were suffering from hunger and threats of invasion, told Jeremiah when he pleaded with them to turn to God.

We will do whatever we want. We will burn incense and pour out liquid offerings to the Queen of Heaven just as much as we like—just as we, and our ancestors, and our kings and officials have always done in the towns of Judah and in the streets of Jerusalem. For in those days, we had plenty to eat, and we were well off and had no troubles!

Who is this Queen of Heaven? Scholars and archaeologists agree that she was considered the wife of God Jehovah, who gave birth to a son, Tammau. She is believed to be the goddess, Asteroth, known by many other names, including, Asharah, Venus, and Anat. Pouring out drink offerings meant pouring wine and having a little orgy in the name of worship of Asteroth. Jeremiah was commanding the people to return to a true worship of God. But the people of Israel said: "*When we worshipped God, we almost starved to death. But when we worshipped the Queen of Heaven, we had plenty.*"

What they were saying is what many people may be saying now.

Christianity isn't working, I am still off work, my family is suffering from COVID-19. We are on public aid, and where is God? The government said they would take care of us. They will feed us, they will see that we have enough. We will find a god who can take care of us and give us what we want.

Many people are worshipping God for what they can get out of it. If God doesn't provide their prosperity, they will just go and find a god who will.

They will be ripe for the enemy's own little harvest of souls. He will be adorned and presented as the Queen of Heaven, who will give them plenty.

There is a rabbinical story of a rabbi who was asked to pray for a man in need. The rabbi agreed and went to God, asking that God meet the need of this man. God said He would, but this rabbi would lose his inheritance in the world to come if He did. The rabbi agreed to give up his inheritance in the world to come if God would answer this man's prayer. When he told the man that God would answer his prayer, the man rejoiced and asked, *"How did this come about?"* The rabbi replied that he had to forfeit his inheritance in the world to come. The man said: *"Oh, rabbi, I never intended for you to have to make such a sacrifice."*

The rabbi replied:

> *It was no sacrifice. All my life I wondered if I was serving God to find a secure place in the world to come. Now that I know I will not have such a place, I can be sure that any service I do for God will be out of love and not personal gain.*

The God Jehovah of Judaism and Christianity offers something that other religions' gods do not offer – love. Other gods have to buy their devotion and worship. God Jehovah does not have to purchase our love. He does not have to dangle prosperity, good health, great relationships, and a heavenly home. We can love Him even if poverty and poor health come. As Andre Crouch once sang: *"If heaven was never promised to me, it would still be worth having the Lord in my life."*

11

DALA' SEVERIN

Psalms 56:2-3: *"I am constantly hounded by those who slander me, and many are boldly attacking me. But when I am afraid, I will put my trust in you."* (Living Bible)

The real persecution we will face in the future will be slander and lies. The psalmist, who was most likely David, was under constant attack, not against his physical well-being, but against his emotional well-being. Slander, lies, and attacks on your reputation will quickly wear you down, and eventually put you out of God's business.

My father used to tell the story of the day Satan decided to retire. He had a big garage sale and priced all of his tools to reflect that particular tool's value. He had lust; that brought a high price. He had daily cares; which did not bring such a high price, particularly since that often led people to God. Persecution, martyrdom, church burnings, and Bible burning did not fetch such a high price either They drove more people to God than away from Him. He had anger, fear, and all the other tools he used to draw people away from God. But there was one tool that held the highest price. This tool did not draw people to God, and it was a sure-fire way to keep people from serving God.

By the end of the day, all of his tools were sold except for this one, because it had such a high price. Satan looked at it and realized that he could stay in business with just this one tool. So he started using it in earnest, and is still using that tool today. The tool is called *discouragement.*

Churches will be accused of hate speech. Pastors will face scandal. The media will make it sound like every preacher is a pedophile.

This evil will be unmasked in the coming months. Churches will close their doors. Pastors will leave the ministry, because they are just too tired of trying to make a go of it. There will be more and more criticism of the church. Slanders, and lies will be spread in the media. Churches will be accused of hate speech. Pastors will face scandal. The media will make it sound like every preacher is a pedophile.

I was in a coffee shop not too long ago. I overheard a conversation between a youth pastor and a teenager. This youth pastor was encouraging the teenager, who was going through a difficult time. They prayed together and shared scripture. The youth pastor led this young man to the Lord. Then they shared a hug.

When they left, a woman sitting behind me leaned over and asked. *"Did you hear and see that? Will you be a witness when I call the police?"*

I was shocked. *"Call the police?"* I asked, *"For what?"*

The woman looked at me with disgust, and said, *"You saw and heard with your own eyes and ears. That man thinks he is a preacher, but he is a pedophile and needs to be stopped."* The enemy doesn't need to outlaw religion when he has slander and lies to destroy its leadership. If we risk being accused of hate speech or being a predator when we share the gospel, our faith will diminish quickly.

One morning while reading through ancient Jewish literature, written around the time of Jesus, I ran across an old Aramaic phrase that sounded familiar. It should; I grew up with it. The Midrash phrase was, *"In such an hour that you think not the Shekinah glory will come."* What it reminded me of was Matthew 24:44: *"Therefore be ye also ready: for in such an hour as ye think not the Son of man cometh."* This was a familiar phrase among the religious Jews, and possibly among the disciples during the time of Jesus. In fact, the Aramaic words in the first-century *dabashatha dala severin (in a moment that you do not think)* is an old Aramaic idiomatic expression that dates long before Jesus was born on this earth.

I am not saying Jesus was not talking about his return, but remember, everyone listening to Jesus speak these words are long gone. It would make sense that Jesus also had a secondary meaning for those who would not be on earth for his return. If we examine the history of this idiom, we will find a lesson that is at the very root of our survival as we enter this time of testing.

This old Aramaic idiom developed from the picture of a father teaching his child to walk. If his child *did not think (dala severin)* the infant would not stumble. I have to wonder if Jesus was using this old rabbinic phrase to teach us something for any period in history. If so, then the disciples may have heard something quite different. In fact, they may have taken a meaning totally the opposite of what we understand when we read Matthew 24:44. Our thinking or what we have been taught, is that the return of Jesus would be unexpected. We view this as the primary message, but I suggest that it is the secondary message. The disciples heard the primary message, which most of us may never hear. This would suggest that God is preparing us to bring a message of peace and healing to the world we live in today.

In the coming days, the enemy is taking off his mask to blatantly, in our faces, call good evil and evil good.

In the coming days, the enemy is taking off his mask to blatantly, in our faces, call good evil and evil good. Our message of love and hope will be called a predatory tool or hate speech. As we enter into a period of trouble, *dala severin* will be more important than ever. The message being that like a child, we need to learn to walk; just as we need to first learn to walk in faith and God's power and glory.

When a child learns to walk, his father sets the child a few feet from him, steps back, opens his arms, and says, *"Come here, and Daddy will give you a hug."* The child is so anxious for that hug that he forgets he doesn't know how to walk. He *dala severin*. He does not think about walking because his focus is on Daddy and that hug. When he gets that hug, he suddenly realizes: *"Well, what do you know I don't have to crawl. I can get to Daddy on two legs like the grown-ups. How cool is that? I think I will try that again."*

In this process of learning to walk in God's power and glory, we are going to stumble, we are going to fall, and we will get bruised and hurt, but keep in mind that that is just part of the process of learning to walk. At the moment we fall and stumble the heavenly Father picks us up, comforts us, and tell us, *"It's okay, let's try this again."*

Peter experienced this very thing when he was *learning to walk* on water. Once a child starts thinking: *"Hey, I'm walking…"* He will suddenly stumble. But so long as he keeps his eyes focused on his father, anticipating that hug, he will walk without stumbling. Did Peter have this ancient rabbinic teaching in mind when he attempted to walk on water? Once he stopped thinking about Jesus *(dala severin)* and thought, *"This is not possible."* he began to sink. According to the ancient teaching, the Shekinah glory will come when you *dala severin* in other words, *when you stop thinking and just focus on God.*

Learning to walk is the process of entering the hour when you *dala severin (think not).* It is the process of learning to clear your mind of all thoughts except those of Jesus and being focused on

Him. Jesus instructed His disciples, who would go through great tribulations as they spread the gospel, in an exercise to help them survive. He is instructing us the same today. We will face a great temptation to compromise by not sharing the gospel in these last days.

It is not easy to put your entire focus on God, for every time you do, the worldly thoughts and problems come in, and you stumble. Like Peter, when you take your eyes off Jesus, you begin to sink. Peter was doing just fine walking on water because he was only thinking about that hug from Jesus. Then he started to look around, see the waves and the storm, and that is when that old computer in his head began to calculate. *"I am walking on water. That is not possible and, oh my, look at this storm."* He took his eyes off of Jesus for just a moment, and he was crying out to Jesus to help him.

But like that loving father with his arms open to give his child a big hug, He fully understands we are still learning to walk. He reaches down with a loving hand and picks us up as we are sinking into the waters, reminding us that we must continue to have faith. When Jesus said, *"O ye of little faith."* He wasn't speaking in frustration: *"Oh, I don't know what I am going to do with you people you have such little faith, how will you ever manage."*

When I read this in the Aramaic, the language Jesus spoke, I get a picture of Jesus saying, *"Look at you, look what you accomplished with just a little faith. Can you imagine what you will be able to do with whole bunches of faith?"*

Jesus said the same thing when he calmed the storm. *"You had just enough faith to call on me and believe I was capable of doing something. Can you imagine if you expand that little faith you have?"*

Consider the fact that Peter was walking on water. No, that is not a little faith. If that was little faith, then my faith can only be seen under a microscope. The word *little* in the Aramaic found in Matthew 14:31 and again in Matthew 8:26 to His disciples, is the word *z'or*, which means to diminish, to reduce in size. Literally, what Jesus said to Peter was: *"Peter, you have that faith. Look at you, you walked out to Me on water, and then at the last minute you took your eyes off of Me. You looked around, you saw the waves, the churning water, the storm and you z'or your faith; you reduced and diminished your faith."*

Earlier I quoted a rabbi who gave me one of my most treasured pieces of advice: *"Faith is not obtained, it is revealed."* Peter revealed his faith when he jumped out of that boat and onto the water. He did not obtain this faith; it was already there, per Ephesians 2:8 that tells us faith is a gift from God. But once we take our eyes off of Jesus, that *qlippah* begins to develop, that ice shell begins to form. As we continue to shiver in the cold darkness of fear, the water begins to turn to slush and then starts to develop into a hard frozen shell, and our faith begins to *z'or*, diminish.

We listen to the news about a riot in a distant city. The media makes it sound like the entire nation is in flames, when it is just a few blocks in a city you may never visit. We hear the death toll from the pandemic is reaching one million. With seven billion people in the world, that is like .01% of the world's population. Imagine the terror you might have felt if you lived in Europe during the Black Death, where the death toll reached 65% of the population. But people still live in fear. People still tremble at what the future may hold. The more you hear, the more you take your eyes off of Jesus. Now don't get me wrong, God put the ability to be afraid in us. But fear is a blessing and a curse. A blessing as it will remind us to wear our mask and practice social distancing. However, fear can be a curse when we let the enemy plant that fear in us to the point where it interferes with our relationship with God rather than draw us to Him. The enemy knows just the right formula of fear to put within us so we can cross that line that turns a blessing into a curse.

The enemy knows just the right formula of fear to put within us so we can cross that line that turns a blessing into a curse.

No doubt, Peter feared stepping out of that boat to walk on water, so he asked Jesus if it was possible, and Jesus put out his arms and said: *"Come to Me for a big hug."* That thought of a hug from Jesus was enough for him to overcome his fear, to melt that ice that *qlippah* away from his heart, so all he could experience was the love of God. Yet, the enemy knew just the right amount of fear to create that *qlippah*; and all he needed to do was influence Peter to look away from Jesus and see the waves.

Again, let me take you back to Hebrews 3:7-8: *"Wherefore (as the Holy Ghost saith, To day if ye will hear his voice, Harden not your hearts, as in the provocation, in the day of temptation in the wilderness."*

How do you hear God's voice? Remember the story of Elijah in I Kings 19? Old Jezebel was really on Elijah's case and sent a posse out after him, with orders to: *"Bring him back dead or alive, preferably dead."* Elijah hot-tailed it to Mt. Choreb, where he spent 30 days seeking the face of God. God spoke to him in a still small voice and instructed him to step out of the cave he was hiding in. I believe Elijah had a problem similar to that which we have today, and will face soon. A still small voice is okay when you are asking God for a parking place. No big deal, if your signals get crossed, and you don't pick up on that still small voice and lose a parking space. After all, that still small voice is usually just a feeling, a sense, a quickening in your spirit which could easily be your imagination. But when the chips are down and your life, or the lives of your loved ones are at stake, you need more than just a little shiver in your liver. You need God to speak to you as He did to Moses and the people of Israel, in an earthquake, or a mighty wind, or even a burning bush. This cat and mouse game of a still small voice will not cut it.

God told Elijah to step outside his cave where he would experience a great wind, an earthquake, and fire. But look what Elijah found:

> *And, behold, the Lord passed by, and a great and strong wind rent the mountains, and brake in pieces the rocks before the Lord; but the Lord was not in the wind: and after the wind an earthquake; but the Lord was not in the earthquake: And after the earthquake a fire; but the Lord was not in the fire: and after the fire a still small voice.*

(I Kings 19:11-12)

God preferred to not speak to Elijah in an earthquake, wind, or fire, but He wanted to speak to Him in a still small voice. Maybe there is a clue why God chooses to speak in a still small voice when you look at these words in Hebrew. God spoke in a *qol demamah daqah*. The word *qol* is a voice, but in its Semitic root, it is simply expressing a thought. God did not express His thoughts in an earthquake, wind, or fire but in a *demamah daqah*.

The first thing to note is that this is in a feminine form. God is speaking out of His feminine nature, that nurturing, loving, caring, and tender part of Himself. He is not taking the masculine role of a disciplinarian, rebuking Elijah: *"Why do you question me? Quit your belly aching, man up, suck in that gut and stop whining."* God wanted to speak to Elijah gently, not in a violent earthquake, wind or fire, but like a mother gently trying to soothe and calm her crying baby and assure it that all is well, mommy is there.

In Hebrew, the word, *damanah* is from the root word *daman*, which is a stillness, a calm. God wanted to speak to Elijah in a calming voice. The word *daqah,* is a word for gentle. Elijah was having a panic attack. He felt like a failure, he was tired of all this trouble, he just wanted to die, and God spoke to him in gentle, soothing tones. You know there will come a time soon where you will be in a state of panic, facing situations and fears like you never faced before, and you will be screaming out to God: *"Where are you? I need something right now!"* You will be looking for God's voice in an earthquake or maybe a mighty wind or a fire, but all the time he will be whispering to you: *"Hey, I'm here, calm down, everything's cool, I'm in control, it will all be okay. Now look at me, see my arms outstretched, come on, walk in faith to your Heavenly Father for a big hug."*

You will be looking for God's voice in an earthquake or maybe a mighty wind or a fire, but all the time he will be whispering to you

Let's take another look at Matthew 24:44. Does it say that Jesus will return at a time when we do not expect Him? There are millions of Christians eagerly expecting the return of Jesus. I am sure it can be read that way, and that is most likely a secondary meaning. But really, is there ever a moment when no one in this world is expecting the return of Jesus. Is there ever a moment when not one of the many millions of believers is thinking about his return? Not one moment that would give Jesus a brief window of opportunity to slip in His return before someone starts to think about it again?

As I said earlier, everyone Jesus was speaking to then, are long gone to their reward. Why would He bait them with a hint that He was returning in their lifetime? I am not a prophetic teacher, so perhaps there is an answer to these questions, but after 70 years in the evangelical world, I've never heard one, or at least one that was not a real stretch of the imagination.

All I am suggesting is that maybe we look at the other side of this coin. Try to hear what the disciples heard when Jesus used an idiom familiar to them but not to us. He could be talking about to a future generation that will see His second coming. But for those who will not be on earth for that event, He had a primary message which is just as important to us today. Don't jump into faith; start with baby steps. Start your learning process by focusing on Jesus, who has His arms extended saying: *"Come on, Come to me for a hug, don't look at those waves and the powerful wind, just look toward me."*

12

The Lesson of Nineveh

I have a very good idea, based upon my *Time Loop* theory, who the next president will be, or if we will even have a president after the election in November. But, as I keep reminding you, I am not a prophet or watchman. I have no supernatural insight into the future. I am only using Scripture and making a guess that history will repeat itself. By the time you read this, the elections may be over and you'll know anyway.

Since I would only be guessing, I will not share my opinion on the results of the next election because, as I write this, I do not believe that the results are set in stone. Many prophecies do not come to pass, for the simple reason believers heed the warning of the prophets, and God does not have to fulfill the prophecy. Many prophesies are conditional. In fact, my *Time Loop* theory is so conditional that God does not have to repeat history ... if Christians obey Him.

I have another theory, maybe as crazy as my *Time Loop* and *Corkscrew* theories. I believe that there are two timelines. God knows the future, but He also knows the *possible* futures. Two possible timelines. One, in which we submit to God, and another in which we do not.

Years ago, when I graduated from seminary, I had a dream that I believe came from God. God showed me two different futures for my life. One was that I would be a pastor of a big church with bestselling books, television ministry, and appearances in high places. Then He showed me the same man, now old and tired, crying out to God; weeping because he never felt a deep close relationship with God. The Lord told me that this would be my life if I chose.

Then he showed me another timeline; one in which I struggled all my life, going through some very painful and heartbreaking experiences, never having a successful ministry, as the world views success. This man, in his later years was filled the joy of the Lord, experiencing a deep abiding faith and love for Him.

I distinctly remember hearing the words, *"Choose you this day whom you will serve."* I chose the latter, and boy, I tell you, it was every bit as painful, heartbreaking, and difficult as I saw in my dream. But because of that, as David said: *"If not for my affliction, I would not have sought the Lord."* Take me back to that day when I had to make my choice, and I would not hesitate to make the same decision.

Is the future set in stone? Did God lay everything out in advance? Are all of our prayers and fasting just exercises in futility?

Is the future set in stone? Did God lay everything out in advance? Are all of our prayers and fasting just exercises in futility? When God told Israel, as they entered the Promised Land, that he would give them a blessing and a curse, he gave them the power of choice. The power to change the future or shape the future. God's will was for Israel to enter the Promised Land forty years earlier, but the people made the wrong choice and turned the blessing to a curse. They chose a different timeline, but they eventually ended up in the Promised Land. Let me use the City of Nineveh as an example.

Nineveh was a powerful trade center whose origins date back to 6,000 BC. Between 3,000 – 2,000 BC, Nineveh it was a major religious center for the worship of the goddess Ishtar. Around 1,273-1,244 BC, King Shalmaneser I turned Nineveh into a powerful political force. By 1,000 BC, major building projects started in Nineveh. It was a powerful trade center and political base in the region.

Jonah prophesied in Nineveh around 762 BC. Keep in mind these dates are approximate and can be challenged. However, this is a generally accepted date when God called Jonah to prophesy to Nineveh, that if they did not repent, the city would be destroyed. Politically, there was a 300-year power struggle for Nineveh between the Hittites, Matanni, Hatti, and the Assyrians until about 722, when King Sargon II of Assyria secured the territory for the Assyrian Empire. His son Sennacherib moved the capital of the Assyrian Empire to Nineveh after the death of his father around 705 BC. Nineveh entered its most glorious time for the next 100 years or so until the Babylonians conquered it in 612 BC.

Jonah's prophesy would have taken place during the 300 years of turmoil. During this time, Nineveh was not a capital city of any one empire. It was usually ruled by a governor, appointed by the power in control of the city at the time. Our English translations refer to the king of Nineveh in the Book of Jonah. However, the Hebrew word, *melek* for king has a wide range of use and could easily apply to a governor. The governor at this time was likely a man named *Nabu-mukin-ahi*. We know little about him except his name appears to be Akkadian, given to him by the Assyrians who opposed him and were threatening to invade the city and destroy it. As this was a turbulent time for the city, it is not surprising that Jonah's message was well received. The violence in the streets were most likely by revolutionaries and terrorists financed by the Assyrians to soften up the city for invasion. I would liken it to the takeover of portions of Portland, Oregon by radicals we witnessed in the past year, and the riots we have seen in the streets.

Such actions brought fear and terror to the people of Nineveh. Some historians believe that the city's major god at this time was Dagon, the fish god. That might have given added incentive to the people of Nineveh when a man who spent three days in a fish's belly appeared in the city preaching of coming destruction. Three days of having his skin and hair eaten away by the acids in the fish's stomach was enough to add truth to Jonah's story. A giant fish likened to their god Dagon had swallowed him, and his God, Jehovah rescued him.

Terrorists and revolutionaries were already running through the streets destroying business, looting and defying local authorities.

You can imagine the terror the people of Nineveh felt. Here is a God more powerful than the god they are hoping will defend them; and this God is saying that they will be destroyed unless they repent. Terrorists and revolutionaries were already running through the streets destroying business, looting and defying local authorities. There's talk of another power invading their city. The people of Nineveh were crying out to their god, Dagon, to save them Then here comes this man, walking into their city, looking like a zombie with this amazing story of how his God Jehovah spared him from their god so he could bring a message to them. If they did not repent, there would be a major civil war in that city in 40 days. That scene would scare the living pudding out anyone. It's enough to make anyone repent!

Well, repent they did. Even the governor repented in sackcloth and ashes. People called out to God, Jehovah to spare their land, which He did. A great revival took place. History is sort of blank for the next fifty or so years, but it appears Nineveh entered a period of prosperity and when Sargon II stabilized the area, and Nineveh became one of the greatest cities in the world.

This is a clear case of fear that could become a blessing or a curse. We are living in a time of fear, fear for the survival of our nation, fear for the economy, fear for our health. It is up to believers as to whether this fear will be a blessing and bring about a revival, or a curse and draw us away from God, allowing a *qlippah* to form around our hearts. If Christians are looking to the next election for salvation, they are looking in the wrong direction. No matter who gets elected, judgment has been declared on this nation.

I don't know which candidate God will use, I can guess, but I believe God has a timeline laid out for either candidate. One will bring us to destruction. Another will bring us to a revival, like the one in Nineveh. Nineveh would have been destroyed if the people had not repented. God had two timelines for that city. One if they didn't repent, leading to destruction, and one if they did repent, leading to revival.

What we must not do, is try to decide _how_ God is going to deliver us. He may just do it through the presidential candidate you think will least likely deliver us. Our job is to not look to the left or look to the right. Not to watch the polls or the news media, but focus our attention on God. Keep our eyes on Him and listen to that soothing, gentle voice telling us that all will be okay regardless of what happens. And by the way, there is a candidate God would like to see win. So, be sure to vote as you follow His still, small, gentle, soothing, comforting voice. But don't worry, even if judgment comes, you'll be okay. Just don't take your eyes off of God.

The point is that the leader of this nation has not already been decided. No prophet can tell us who it will be. But, if this nation will humble itself, seek the face of God, and pray, He will heal our land and shift the timeline to one of healing rather than one of destruction.

The point is that the leader of this nation has not already been decided. No prophet can tell us who it will be.

There was a transition of power in Nineveh, but it was a peaceful transition from what we find so far in our historical research. Right now, much of the spiritual power in this country has fallen into the hands of the enemy, but our repentance, prayer, and fasting will give us a peaceful transition of that particular power.

13

A Timeline Into 2021

Again, I am not a prophet nor the son of a prophet. I am not a watchman. I have no supernatural insights. I am only a scribe, a dusty old professor, who loves history and likes to play around with timelines. I am offering a possible timeline into the future, for your consideration only. Perhaps, it might serve to encourage you to spend more time before God in prayer and fasting, more time drawing closer to Him. If I accomplish that, then this book will have fulfilled its purpose.

I see many parallels to the United States and the First Persian Empire, which existed for approximately 220 years.

Let's begin our timeline here:

(Keep in mind these dates for the Persian Empire are approximate and disputed.)

- First Persian Empire approximately 550 BC

- Destruction of the First Empire approximately 330 BC

- Length of the first Empire approximately 220 years

- Approximate start of the United States 1783 + 220 = 2003 220 years

- America's peace treaty was signed with Britain in 1783, which could mark the beginning of the United States as a nation. But then maybe the adoption of the Declaration of Independence in 1776, or the ratification of the Constitution in 1788 could mark the beginning of the United States.

- 2003 could have been a designated time on one of God's timelines for the fall of the United States. 2001 was certainly a test, showing that the people of this country were willing to turn to God in a time of national trouble. This country experienced a period of revival after 9/11.

- God may have shifted his timeline and granted the United States a period of grace, just as He gave Nineveh a period of grace when they turned to God.

- 25 is a Biblical number of grace upon grace. Could God be giving us 25 more years of grace until 2026?

Let's look a little further at the history of the Persian Empire.

- In 539 BC, Cyrus brings an end to the Babylonian Empire and installs Persian rule.

- Daniel finds favor with Cyrus, when he shows Cyrus that the Prophets named him by name as one who would favor the Jewish people and aid in their return to the Promised Land. Three years later, in 536 BC, Daniel has a terrifying vision, or dream of the future, and prays for understanding.

- Cambyses, the prince of Persia, governs the city of Babylon for nine-months, until his father removes him. Cambyses begins plotting his next move. During this time, Daniel prays for understanding. The messenger sent to Daniel is delayed as he tries to influence the prince of Persia in his next move.

- Eight years after Cambyses' removal from his position in Babylon (530 BC), his father, Cyrus, dies in a campaign at the North East frontier, and Cambyses becomes the sole ruler of

Persia. He immediately sets out to conquer Egypt, where he is successful, and spends the next eight years establishing his rule in Egypt, adopting the Egyptian religion, and the worship of the goddess *Neit*. On his way back to Persia to continue his role as king and establish the worship of the goddess *Neit* as the state religion in 522 BC, he learns that his brother has staged a coup and set himself up as the king of Persia. Whether in battle or attempted suicide, Cambyses is wounded in the thigh and dies a few days later from infection. On his deathbed, he is said to have confessed that he murdered his brother and that the present king was an imposter.

- Darius, who was plotting to take the throne for himself, declares that the king is a fraud and stages another coup, setting himself up as the new king of Persia. This prevented the establishment of a state religion based upon a pagan goddess, paving the way for the Jews to receive favor from the king, and return to their land.

- In 2008 a president of the United States was elected who showed little favor to the Jewish nation and aided their enemies. His chosen successor, eight years later, who was almost guaranteed to win the election, and continue to diminish the United States' role in their support of Israel. She lost the election in what many felt was like a coup. Donald Trump, a major supporter of Israel, took office, becoming a parallel to Darius I, an outsider who many believed, had no business in the White House.

- During his first term, the United States military might increased; just like Persia's empire became a world-class military power under Darius. Darius was met with much opposition. He was accused of being an outsider and not of the royal family. There were many coup attempts, but Darius miraculously held his office. Darius' name means *"he who holds firm the goodness."*

- During the first four years of the Trump presidency, he faced much opposition and numerous attempts to remove him from office. Miraculously, all these attempts failed. Trump's name in Hebrew would be *chatzar*, which means *"one who holds things together."*

On the negative side, Darius started a conflict with the empire of Greece. His successors were so focused on these events and internal problems that they failed to give any support to the Jews in the Promised Land, leading up to a war of Independence led by the Maccabees. There is no mention of Persia, as it was in a state of decline on the world stage.

Should we follow a similar timeline, Trump will again lead this nation, to retain its status as a superpower, restore our economy, and bring Israel into a time of freedom and power. He may also start a feud with a powerful nation that will eventually bring the United States into a state of decline, such that Israel will be left to fend for themselves.

But that timeline not set in stone. Our grace period could very well end in approximately 2026. Then again, it may not, and none of this may happen. We could just keep plugging along as we have been.

Again, I am not a prophet, and I have no supernatural inspiration, vision, or dream. I only have history and God's Word. Neither gives exact dates or precise timelines. I am not a biblical prophecy student, so I have no idea how this would fit the timelines of popular prophetic teachers. I deliberately avoid reading articles or books by prophecy teachers because I don't want to unintendedly be influenced by them.

My dates are approximate. My glimpse of the future is guesswork. The only thing I can speak with surety, is that the next president has not been decided. God has two timelines (maybe more), one for each candidate. Which one will lead us to a period of grace or destruction is not known, perhaps neither, as our future will not be decided by who is in office. God has shown in His Word, and in history, that the direction of a nation is in His hands, and the choices His people make. He can use a man claiming to be a god, like the Pharaoh, a tyrant like Nebuchadnezzar, a rascal like Cambyses, or a usurper like Darius. But He cannot do it without the power of prayer. The release of our wills, through prayer, to God's will on a field where weapons are the power of influence and ammunition is the will of the people.

So what about the 2020 elections?

Well, let's take a deeper look into the history of Persia during the reign of Darius, which seems very similar to America during the presidency of Donald Trump.

The accounts of Darius' rise to the throne were given by the Greek historians Herodotus and Ctesais, and is derived from official versions; but it is interwoven with legend. According to Herodotus, it was Darius who killed Bardiva's impersonator. Darius was a bodyguard for Cambyses when he was in Egypt, but it is believed he returned to Persia to continue his plot to seize the throne with the help of the Medes. With the help of six Persian nobles, he killed the impostor posing as Bardiva. In an earlier chapter, I explained that Bardiva was the rightful heir to the throne but was murdered by his brother Cambyses, so he could become the king. When Cambyses died returning to Persia, Darius claimed to be restoring the kingship to the rightful Achaemenid house. It is doubtful that Darius was a member of the Achaemenid house and merely dummied up his resume. Many historians doubt that he was the rightful heir under the Achaemenid house. Darius was looked upon as an outsider who seized the throne. There were many attempted coups but all miraculously failed. As a result, Darius never did get general recognition as the legitimate king of Persia.

This is much like President Trump, who was an outsider and suffered many attempts to remove him from his office by a deep state loyal to his predecessors. Like Darius, many have not recognized Trump as the legitimate President.

Strengthening his army. weakened by Cambyses, Darius managed to consolidate and strengthen Persia's international powers during his reign. He had many ambitious, far-sighted projects to promote trade and commerce, making Persia an economic power. In 519 BC, he authorized the Jews to rebuild the Temple in Jerusalem. This was in accordance with an earlier decree of Cyrus but never carried out until Darius. Darius officially recognized Jerusalem as the capital city of Judah.

Similarly, President Trump established an American Embassy in Jerusalem, officially recognizing Jerusalem as the Capital of Israel. Something promised by his predecessors but never carried out until Trump became President. I have a coin that shows a picture of President Trump and Cyrus on one side, and the third temple on the other side to commemorate this occasion. Although Cyrus never carried out the plan to help the Jews return to their land, his successor Darius did carry it out.

History notes Darius as an Architect, whose building projects reflected a style that remained unchanged until the end of the empire. Trump is a builder who has assumed a style of Architecture in this country and other nations, which will remain unchanged for many years to come. He has brought a metaphorical style of building within the government that will have a lasting effect. Both Darius and Cambyses have one thing in common; they both died or were unable to complete their goals for the Persian Empire.

I believe in the parallels we are seeing between the Persian Empire and the United States at this time and stage in history would suggest that no matter who wins the election in 2020, the next President will not complete his full term in office.

What I do see coming in 2021 takes no prophet. The ease of closing churches, the spread of lies, the calling of good evil and evil good, turning the gospel of Jesus Christ into hate speech, are all signs of a coming persecution. If a bookworm, like me, who buries himself in his dusty old library, can see it coming, I am sure many others see it coming in their spirits as well. They hear the still small voice, saying, *"The time is coming to choose who you will serve. Will you share my love and gospel at the risk of being called a hater, or will you play it safe and keep quiet?"*

God is once again going to test this nation as He did in 2001. It will have been twenty years since 2001, since this nation was last tested, and turned to God. It is time to test the waters and see if we are ready for another 25 years of grace upon grace. Only this time, the test will be an attack coming from within the nation. It will come in the form of persecution, not physically violent, but a persecution of lies, slander, and censorship. God will be testing the nation of believers to see if they care more for their reputations, their wealth, prosperity, and their security than they do for Him. Will they turn their eyes on Him and walk those waters of faith or will they look at the storm of criticism, threats to their security and comfortable lifestyle? Will they compromise their faith in return for favor with the enemy?

The future of our nation does not rest with the person sitting in the Oval Office. It lies with the Miss Betty's of this nation who are on their knees, storming heaven with the power of the prayers of the righteous.

14

Bonus Chapter: A Bible Code Prediction For 2021

I realize I hedged my bets on my predictions. You probably purchased this book hoping for some good rock-solid predictions, without the maybes, possiblies, and could-be's. Okay, I do have a firm prediction, at least the best I can do without any claim to prophetic gifts. But, I believe the Bible does have some secret codes that give us a clue to the future.

I've been in love with secret codes since I was a child. I longed to be a member of Jet Jackson's secret squadron. Each week my childhood hero, Jet Jackson, gave a coded message that only those who had the secret squadron's decoder badge could understand. Unfortunately, my mother could not afford the sponsor's chocolate drink with the label you needed to send in to get the decoder badge. I did not become a member of the Secret Squadron. Thus, I was left to try and crack the code on my own, to discover what would happen to Jet Jackson and his sidekick Icabod Mudd in the next episode. I had little success. The messages I decoded never occurred in the next episode. So, this failure at cryptography has probably led me to my present-day interest in breaking Bible codes. I pray I am a little more successful here.

The code I am using is called the *Gematria*. This uses numbers to find a hidden message in the Bible, or to find a relationship between one Hebrew word and another. You see, every letter in the Hebrew Alphabet is also a number. For instance, the *Aleph* is the number one. The *Beth* is the number 2. The *Gimmel* is number three, and so forth. Every word in the Hebrew language has a numerical value. For example, the word father is *Aleph Beth*. The *Aleph* is 1 plus the *Beth*, which is 2, equals a numerical value of three. During a Passover Seder, the father will ask his children, *"Who knows three?"* The children would answer, the three fathers; Abraham, Isaac, and Jacob. Every father must attempt to incorporate the characteristics of the three fathers. The *Aleph* is for one God. The *Beth* stands for the home. It is the father's duty to introduce the oneness of God into his home.

There is a biblical reference to the use of the Gematria in Revelation 18:13, we read: *"Here is wisdom. Let him that hath understanding count the number of the beast: for it is the number of a man; and his number [is] Six hundred threescore [and] six".*

One needs wisdom and understanding to count. The word count in Greek is *psephisato*, which means to compute or calculate the number of the beast, which is 666. That is using the Gematria. It uses the numerical value of the beast's name to arrive at some hidden knowledge or secret about the beast, possibly to even identify the beast.

Rabbi Benjamin Blech wrote a book entitled *The Secrets of Hebrew Words*, published by Rowman and Littlefield Publishers in Lanham, Maryland. He gives another example, where he tells how Jewish rabbis, long before Israel's founding as a modern nation, sought to discover if the Bible predicted when the Jews would return to their homeland. They took the Hebrew word from the Torah, *tashuvu*, which means *"you shall return."* It is the word *return* in a Qal Imperfect form. The word is spelled *Taw*, which equals 400, *Shin*, which equals 300, *Beth*, which equals 2, and *Vav*, which equals 6, giving us a total of 708. The rabbis then added to this the millennia, which is 5. Five is the letter *Hei* which Deuteronomy 32:6 uses as an abbreviation for God's name YHWH, so we have God will return you to Israel. Thus, you have the Jewish year 5708. On the Julian calendar that we follow, 5708 is 1948, which is the year that Israel became a nation. How about that? The orthodox Jews knew the exact year they would return to Israel by using the Hebrew numbering system.

That looked like a lot of fun. So, for the sake of this book, old Chaim Bentorah wondered when the great revival that we are predicting will take place. I used the word

I get the Jewish Calendar year of the next great revival at 5781, which happens to be on our Julian Calendar September 2020 – September 2021.

salvation for revival as that is what a revival amounts to, people getting saved in mass. I needed to use the word salvation in a Hiphil perfect form and the *Hei* for God to express the words that God has sent salvation or a revival. The word for salvation in Hebrew is in a Hiphal form as *hosha'ah*. *Hosah'ah* is spelled with the *Hei* = 5, *Shin* = 300, the *Vav* = 6, the *Ayin* = 70 and the *Taw* = 400 which totals 781. I add the millennia of 5 to represent God bringing this revival, and I get the Jewish Calendar year of the next great revival at 5781, which happens to be on our Julian Calendar September 2020 – September 2021.

But let's not stop there. Back in 1909, two men, Charles Parham and William Seymour, were part of the Azusa Street Revival, and considered the fathers of the modern-day Pentecostal outpouring. They gave the same prophecy, at the same time, without either one knowing they were giving the same prophecy. Charles Parham gave his prophecy on the East Coast, and William Seymour gave his prophecy on the West Coast. Both were identical. Both prophesied that in 100 years from 1909, there would be the former and latter rain outpouring or revival, and it would not be local like Azusa street. This revival would sweep the nation, and it would bring the black and white community together in praise and worship.

Well, one hundred years have passed twelve years ago, but no revival. Most people debunk this prophecy. Yet, there was much tension in the city of Ninevah twelve years before Jonah's arrival, with his prophecy of the coming destruction. During this time, three kingdoms were fighting for control of Nineveh. Nineveh's ruler didn't know one day from the next if he would be the ruler or even alive. There were radicals in the streets, creating violence, and people were afraid to go out of their homes. Then comes this prophet, who says that unless they repent to the Hebrew God, Jehovah, their city would be destroyed. Well, we know the story, they repented, and the city was spared, not only that, there was a great revival.

I believe there was a twelve-year period of sorrow before this revival.

History is pretty muddled, but, from my research, I believe there was a twelve-year period of sorrow before this revival. There is usually a period of sorrow or trouble before a great revival. Twelve years ago, in the 2008 – 2009 period, this nation went through the Great Recession. People lost their retirements, their homes, their jobs. Many lost a fortune on the stock market. It was one of the worst economic collapses since the Great Depression. In 2016, there was a political polarization, unlike any in the history of this country since the Civil War. Families and friends split because of political differences. Many families could not even come together for Thanksgiving because of the anger and hatred between families and friends over political views.

We have now entered a pandemic period where there have been lockdowns causing many businesses to go bankrupt, job losses, and fears. We have faced a summer of violent riots and hatred in the streets, and between races. I would say we have had twelve years of sorrow. I focus on the word *sorrow* because it is the word, *d'abah* in Hebrew, which is spelled *Daleth* = 4, Aleph = 1, *Beth* =

2, and *Hei* = 5 for a total of 12 or twelve years of sorrow. Revival often comes after a time of great sorrow, fear, and everything else wrapped up in the word, *d'abah*. Ah, but if we look at this word in the Aramaic and remove the *Daleth*, which could be a prefix for a definite article, we have the word, *'abah*, which means to conform, to compromise. I believe, here is a clue as to what will happen before this revival. There will be such persecution on the church that we will be strongly tempted to *'abah*, compromise our beliefs for acceptance and security. That will be the enemy's major weapon to defeat this coming revival.

***

Final thought

Will Christians be strong and stand for their faith? Will they be willing to suffer persecution and rejection for their faith? Jesus said we would be hated for His sake (Matthew 10:22-24). I see persecution for our faith coming with this next great revival. On September 26, 2020, Franklin Graham held a prayer march on the mall of Washington DC with 100,000 people praising God and praying for this nation. It was not reported by the mainstream news media; it was almost like a news blackout. Yet, the revival is beginning, despite the enemy's attempts to silence it.

About the Author

Chaim Bentorah is the pseudonym of a Gentile Christian who taught college-level Biblical Hebrew and is an Amazon Bestselling Author. He prepared his students to take the placement exams for graduate school. He has now developed a method of study where he can prepare any Believer, regardless of age or academic background, to study the Word of God using Biblical Hebrew.

Chaim Bentorah received his B.A. degree from Moody Bible Institute in Jewish Studies and his M.A. degree from Denver Seminary in Old Testament and Hebrew and his PhD in Biblical Archeology. His Doctoral Dissertation was on the "Esoteric Structure of the Hebrew Alphabet." He has taught Classical Hebrew at World Harvest Bible College for thirteen years and also taught Hebrew for three years as a language course for Christian Center High School. He is presently teaching Biblical Hebrew and Greek to pastors in the Metro Chicago area.

www.chaimbentorah.com

Other books by Chaim Bentorah

- Ten Words That Will Change Everything You Know About God
- Does The Bible Really Sat That?
- Treasures of the Deep
- Learning God's Love Language
- Learning God's Love Language Workbook
- Hebrew Word Study: Revealing The Heart Of God
- Journey into Silence
- Whom My Soul Loves
- Intimacy With God
- Is This Really Revival?
- Biblical Truths From Uncle Otto's Farm

Learn Hebrew Word Study
from Chaim Bentorah!
Special introductory offer (Just $0.99 your first month!)

**Do you want to go further in your Hebrew word study?
Join Chaim Bentorah's HebrewWordStudy.com**

Just imagine, having all this at your fingertips, on demand!

- More than 1000 Hebrew studies: $249.00 value
- Hebrew Alphabet poster (download): $10 value.
- 8-hour video Hebrew Word Study Course: $50 value
- 9 Chaim Bentorah e-books free! $90 Value
- Learning God's Love Language audio: $24.99 value
- Weekly live-stream teaching: $499 value
- 24/7 access: "Ask Chaim": $199 value
- Video Hebrew word studies: $499 value
- Hebrew Alphabet video teaching: $50 Value
- 20% off insider discount on Chaim Bentorah books.
- and much more – this just keeps growing!

Visit www.HebrewWordStudy.com